The Woman's Book of

Empowerment

& Confidence

365 Daily Affirmations

Rebekah,
What a year
this will be!.. I hope
2014 is one of your best
yet!. Much love,
Kim

Edited by Linda Ellis Eastman

⚜ *Professional Woman Publishing*
Prospect, Kentucky

The Woman's Book of Empowerment & Confidence
Copyright © 2013 by Linda Ellis Eastman
All rights reserved.

Published by:
Professional Woman Publishing
Post Office Box 333
Prospect, KY 40059
(502) 228-0906
www.pwnbooks.com

Please contact the publisher for quantity discounts.

ISBN 13: 978-0-9897079-3-0

Library of Congress Cataloging-In-Publication Data

Photo credits: Amandee/Dreamstime.com

Printed in the United States of America

INTRODUCTION

May the words contained within this book start each day by bringing you peace, hope and joy. Each co-author has provided a day-by-day Affirmation to reflect upon. Savor each page with your morning coffee or with a quiet meditation time for self-reflection.

May you enjoy this 365 daily affirmation book as much as we enjoyed writing and publishing it.

Linda Ellis Eastman

FOREWORD

Have you ever taught a freshman class at a college or university? The students that reside on campus are excited about being away from their parents. Most express they are looking forward to doing things on their own. The campus layout facilitates for them a perception of living the dreams of their life for the next four years. Zoning on campus is clearly defined with important areas designated for eating, sleeping, exercising and studying. Everything is paid for an exciting place to reside!

Conversely, there are some students who continue to reside with their parents at home. In addition, they have to continue to share in the chores, have to find a part-time job, attend college part-time and get distracted by other things they may have to do during college and work. They have boundaries and curfews as they are not in their own place. The zoning and layout is not that easily navigated as they may have siblings at home who depend on them to do things for them.

Well, this is not unique to college students as it applies to adults as well. The commonality of situations like these is that you have to Empower Yourself on your journey of life. Success does not just happen; you have to work at it. How is your life going? Are you where you want to be? Does your life reflect a plan for the next one, three or five years? Do you have the confidence needed to move to your next level of success? Oprah Winfrey said, "I would rather be prepared and never selected, than to be selected and not prepared."

When you combine Empowerment and Confidence and make daily affirmations a part of your daily routine, the results will be success. It will keep you focused and encourage you to be better and not bitter - because you remained in the same situation year after year. The great news is, you don't have to take this journey alone. You were predestined to be what God has planned for you. Here is an Empowerment and

Confidence bible verse for you to remember: *"For I know the thoughts that I think towards you, saith the Lord, thoughts of peace, and not evil, to give you an expected end." – Jeremiah 29:11*

Linda Ellis Eastman, founder of the Professional Woman Network and Publishing companies, has empowered thousands of women and men through her seminars, coaching, conferences and books series. She has empowered and instilled confidence in many who are now successful and thriving today in their careers and businesses. The last 9 years with PWN have empowered me to do more for others in their endeavors. For anyone starting a business or retired and rebranding themselves, start with Linda Ellis Eastman at PWN.

I have a purpose and passion for *"Growing & Empowering Future Leaders Now, for Success."* for empowering the next generation of leaders to be the best in their careers, life and relationships. For giving them strategies, transferring knowledge, skills, and abilities. Ms. Eastman and the co-authors of this book share some of my passions reflected in this book. It is an investment in YOU if you read it and inculcate the daily affirmations in *The Woman's Book of Empowerment and Confidence: 365 Daily Affirmations*. Yes, men can read it too. Give yourself a picture of greater potential, there is a deposit of greatness, wealth and healing within you waiting to be developed and released.

Dr. Amicitia Maloon-Gibson,

The Empowerment Doc, www.mgaapdi.com

LINDA ELLIS EASTMAN

Linda Ellis Eastman is President and CEO of The Professional Woman Network (PWN), an International Training and Consulting Organization on Women's Issues. She has designed seminars which have been presented in China, the former Soviet Union, South Africa, the Phillipines, and attended by individuals in the United States from such firms as McDonalds, USA Today, Siemens-Westinghouse, the Pentagon, the Department of Defense, and the United States Department of Education.

An expert on women's issues, Ms. Eastman has certified and trained over two thousand women to start consulting/seminar businesses originating from such countries as Pakistan, the Ukraine, Antigua, Canada, Mexico, Zimbabwe, Nigeria, Bermuda, Jamaica, Costa Rica, England, South Africa, Malaysia, and Kenya. Founded in 1982 by Linda Ellis Eastman, The Professional Woman Network is committed to educating women on a global basis regarding, self-esteem, confidence building, stress management, and emotional, mental, spiritual and physical wellness.

Ms. Eastman has been featured in USA Today and listed in Who's Who of American Women, as well as Who's Who of International Leaders. In addition to women's issues, Ms. Eastman speaks internationally regarding the importance of human respect as it relates to race, color, culture, age, and gender. Annually, she facilitates an international conference where speakers and participants from many nations discuss issues that are unique to women on a global basis.

Linda Ellis Eastman is also founder of The Professional Woman Speakers Bureau and The Professional Woman Coaching Institute. Ms. Eastman has dedicated her businesses to increasing the self-esteem and personal dignity of women and youth around the world.

Contact:
The Professional Woman Network
P.O. Box 333
Prospect, KY 40059
(502) 566-9900
lindaeastman@prodigy.net
www.pwnbooks.com
www.protrain.net

The Woman's Book of

Empowerment & Confidence

JANUARY 1

Who wouldn't want a miracle? Yet, we very rarely ask for miracles. We see miracles as a rarity that only happen once in a very long while. But what if we led our lives in expectation of miracles?

We would know that every day that we breathe is a miracle if we understood the physiology of the body and what it takes for everything to work together so perfectly in order for us to take each and every breath. Pregnant women are miracles when we understand how much it takes for the body, along with timing, in order to conceive. We understand that birth is a daily miracle once we take into consideration the intricacies of conception that form a child.

Every day is a miracle when you think about it! Miracles are all around us. So why do we think miracles are unrealistic? If anything, we should think that anything other than a miracle is unrealistic! Go out and see the miracle of your life and then plan for new miracles every day.

Kymberley Clemons-Jones

JANUARY 2

Be kind to one another, tenderhearted, forgiving one another, as God in Christ forgave you. – Ephesians 4:32

My step mother Mary Agnes Russell Pobst McLeskey was the most amazing person that was kidnapped into our family by my Dad when I was nineteen. I say kidnapped as once you are in, it is more like a life sentence with NO PAROLE. That whole business about we keep what we kill, we take it to heart in my wonderfully loving and daily amusing family! Just saying…..

I remember so many conversations that I have had with her over the years that mean so much to me. She has passed on now but I wanted to share the true meaning of EMPATHY with all you folks that just think you know what it means.

The first one was when Mary Agnes married my Dad, Boyce L. McLeskey and moved into our family home that was on the same road where she lived for many, many years with her family. She invited my Mother to spend the weekend with her and Daddy as everyone remained friends after the divorce. She opened up her home that used to be my mother's home to my mother. She was kind and gracious with no stress.

The second time was when we were discussing the divorce and how hard it had been for my younger sister and me at the time. She was very empathetic in siding with mother on her reasons for instigating the divorce. She helped me to look at the situation from my mother's point of view and see, now that I was an adult, how I would have felt.

Over the years, she gave me so many more examples it was hard not to start thinking with a more empathetic attitude about everyone. So here I am today with a more improved attitude with respect to being empathetic!

Michele McLeskey

JANUARY 3

"Today I give myself permission to be at peace with my emotions."

Emotions control our thinking and behaviour and they also greatly affect our physical bodies. If we ignore or repress our emotions, we are setting ourselves up for unbalanced physical and emotional conditions.

At the same time, emotional reactivity plays into physical and emotional imbalance.

The challenge is to learn to be responsive to situations and events; we can empower ourselves to become responsive as opposed to being reactive.

It is important to be honest about the emotions we are experiencing; in other words – own your emotions and bring them into your conscious awareness. Take a deep breath and, instead of asking "why" (*why is this happening to me...., why is this person making me feel so....*, etc), ask "how" the situation can be re-directed toward a more positive outcome (or ask "what" can be done).

"How" and "What" keep you solution focused and responsive. "Why" has the potential to keep you problem focused and reactive.

Gabriela Eikeland

JANUARY 4

Affirmation: *Today I am being the person of my dreams and desires.*

If you have dreams and goals for your life, one key component to achieving your potential is *being* that person first. It is vital that you begin by adopting the mindset, making the choices and taking the actions of the person you will be when you have the success you desire. Do not wait until you achieve a goal to start to act in alignment with it. The opposite holds true. Be in alignment with what you want to create in order to make it reality.

For example, if you are an at-home entrepreneur aspiring to have a successful 6-figure business, *be* that business person in all that you do and say. If you want to be leaner and fitter, *be* that person who makes healthy food choices and takes time to exercise on a regular basis. If you want to eliminate debt, *be* responsible when you choose how to handle your money. If you want to have more loving, nurturing relationships in your life, *be* a loving and nurturing person.

When you have a dream, a goal, a vision, you also have the power to create it. The key is not to wait for some benchmark achievement to decide that then you can be the person you aspire to be. At some level of your being, you are already that person. You do not need to wait to be all you can be. The key is to be that person now, today, in this moment.

Janet Christensen

JANUARY 5

Affirmation: *"I believe in myself and all I do."*

At the beginning of the year we all like to make *New Year's Resolutions.* Unfortunately for most individuals within a few weeks or a month, we let our resolutions go by the wayside. We soon forget about the commitment we made and move on to something else. Resolutions are nothing more than goals. The key is to make them measurable. This allows us to track the progress of our goal.

The best way to help us stick with a resolution is to determine the path needed to achieve the goal. Next, break it down into smaller attainable action steps. If we plan out the appropriate order for each of the action steps we can also determine when each of the steps will need to be completed. By breaking the resolution up into small steps it will become easier for us to achieve. This will also allow us to celebrate small successes along the way. Attaining small victories will keep us motivated as we continue to move closer to the bigger goal (our resolution).

An additional factor that is important in helping us stick with a resolution is belief. We must have faith in ourselves to achieve our goal. I like the following quote because it helps me to put all of this into perspective: *To accomplish great things, we must not only act, but also dream, not only plan, but also believe.* —Anatole France

Judy Singleton

JANUARY 6

Let your voice be heard.

My daughter's name is Naomi, which means in part, "pleasant, agreeable". On most days this is quite true of her! When she challenges me otherwise, I wonder whether I'm doing her a favor by expecting her to conform to the characteristics that define her name. You see, all my life I've tried to be pleasant and agreeable, fearing that if I offend others with my opinions I would not be loved or respected. I developed much of my belief system based primarily on what I thought others expected me to believe. When it came time to defend my assertions, I was rarely prepared with knowledge; rather, I was only armed with other's opinions and beliefs…not my own. And as a result I felt inadequate and insecure, and I certainly guarded my voice from being heard.

Too many women simply conform rather than stand out due to fear of rejection. As I look at my daughter, I want her to be secure in her convictions and not worry about what others think. This is a delicate balance, as I still believe it is important on the whole to be pleasant and agreeable. After all, most of us would rather spend our time with pleasant people! It is equally as important, though, to let our voice be heard, despite the risk of disagreement.

In what way will you speak your voice today?

Rebecca Sheperd

JANUARY 7

Affirmation: *"You can change your world by changing your words. Remember, life and death are in the power of the tongue".* —Joel Osteen

Do you know people who just say whatever they want? They are negative or always talking about other people. They aren't in the moment and don't think your words can change your life. Keeping a great perspective and authenticity has to do with your words, your thinking and your actions. Words are energy. What comes out of your mouth are your words that you are putting in the universe. Everything has energy. Might as well put out positive words you want to bring back to you. Ideas, great attitude, gratitude, making your dreams come true. It can happen! Take the high road. Try it out; it's sure a better way than taking a back road. Confess over your life what you want and say it out loud. It's fifty times more potent to say it out loud in the universe. For a month say things in a positive way, I challenge you to try it. You may think it's easy but I want you to challenge yourself for a month. See what your life feels like for that month. Miracles do happen!

Angie Schultz

JANUARY 8

Affirmation: *Practice boundaries in your life*

Do your kids get in your purse? Does your daughter get in your closet and borrow things without asking? When your door is closed does the family knock or just walk in? Do they honor you when you're trying to watch your favorite show by not disturbing you? Why do you think boundaries are good? They show honor and respect, and as the Mom it's great to teach your children this before they get into the world. Be the example! Teach your kids by showing them what boundaries are. It helps to keep the peace and not step on anyone's toes. When you honor, respect and have boundaries, it shows what kind of person you are. Sometimes you learn the hard way, by not being respected or honored. Be the change you want to see in your family and the world. Be the BEST you can be. Keep learning. Knowledge is power. There is always room for improvement. "NO" IS A COMPLETE SENTENCE. Saying no is saying yes to yourself. Deal with conflict head on. Set boundaries! Practice setting boundaries with your family, sometimes they are the hardest. You will not only be doing it for you, but you will be showing people how you want to be treated. It's a good thing. It brings a lot more peace to yourself and people around you by knowing what you want and how you want to be treated. It takes leaps of faith! You deserve it!

Angie Schultz

JANUARY 9

Affirmation:
As I nurture my body with alive food,
every cell vibrates its happy dance
and I awaken to the aliveness within me.

Have you ever considered the energetic quality of the food you eat? The more natural and plant-based, the higher the energetic vibration. The more packaged and processed, the lower the vibration.

Because your food nourishes your body, and your body is your vessel through life, you take on the energetic quality of the food you eat. To feel more alive in your life, choose foods that are alive and as close to Mother Nature as possible.

Our bodies were not designed to process man-made chemicals and unnatural substances. While they may make food more convenient and last longer, they deplete our lives of the very goodness Mother Nature supplies in abundance.

Return to the Earth as your Source. Become alive in your life, one bite at a time. You deserve to thrive.

Paula Onysko

JANUARY 10

We are made wise not by the recollection of our past, but by the responsibility for our future. —George Bernard Shaw

The past is the past. What happened cannot be undone and you cannot go back and have a do-over. **You can be paralyzed by your past. Past pain and disappointments can hinder you from moving on with your life** by replaying situations and scenarios that can imprison you.

You cannot do anything about what happened except learn and grow from it. If you have been imprisoned by your past, let today be your turning point. Today can be your day of healing and restoration. **You can break out of the jail of your past and live fully in this present moment.**

I learned this great lesson from my brother, who passed over 20 years ago. He was a proponent of living in the present and enjoying life in the now. You can do the same!

Be inspired to push apart those bars and with boldness and confidence, walk out of the jail of your past and walk into the blessings that are awaiting you.

Affirm: **I release my past and set myself free.**

Frenetta Tate

JANUARY 11

Your net worth to the world is usually determined by what remains after
your bad habits are subtracted from your good ones.
—Benjamin Franklin

At the beginning of the year, we all have new hopes and new dreams. We think about our friends and family that we value, and those we do not value. Often we set new goals and make resolutions to change. It is so easy to think about changes – what would be better if something was different; and, often if someone – else, made changes. We cannot make others change. We cannot change certain things like weather. We cannot move mountains, drain Lake Michigan, or the Atlantic Ocean. We can only change our actions and our thoughts. It is never easy to really change, especially if what we are doing has become a habit.

Shockingly, it takes just 21 days to create a habit, but at least 41 to extinguish a habit. Replacement is possible in some cases, such as drinking herbal tea instead of coffee. Yet, how we feel about those changes can make us have feelings we do not like. For example, going without coffee can cause us to have physical headaches. Liken this to other habits, habits become like comfort food. Our habits, good or bad, comfort us in some way. In some ways we envy those whose habits allow them to be successful. And, we often feel sorry for or pity those whose habits are destructive.

Whether we own a business, have longer term goals of owning a business, having an executive job, or establishing a non-profit to help animals or people who cannot help themselves for some reason, our focus at the New Year, needs to be on how we can prepare to meet those opportunities. To do this, think about using the Strengths Inventory and the Myers-Briggs both free online to help you figure out your strengths and create new habits.

Katrina Everhart

JANUARY 12

Affirmation: *"I know no single formula for success. But over the years
I have observed that some attributes of leadership are universal
and are often about finding ways of encouraging people to combine
their efforts, their talents, their insights, their enthusiasm and
their inspiration to work together."* —Queen Elizabeth II

I have learned many valuable insights about myself through collaborating with others. I have learned my value to the team (my creativity, out-of-the-box thinking and natural leadership ability). I have learned that my strengths differ from those around me. What strengths do you bring to the team? I have learned to actively seek out those differences because I know that our collective diversity makes for a stronger team. I have been exposed to new perspectives, different types of solutions and even different ways of approaching problems through collaboration.

I also know that I don't have a natural tendency to seek out collaboration. I am very independent and action-oriented. Collaboration slows down progress. I have had colleagues who, in my opinion, collaborate too much ensuring that all decisions are made by consensus even when consensus isn't necessary. It's important to strike the delicate balance in order to maximize the effectiveness of collaboration.

In Western society, people are rewarded individually through promotions, raises and special assignments. How does this reward structure hinder collaboration? What does that do to our society's overall success?

Collaboration is often viewed as one of the behavioral strengths of feminine leadership. Effective collaboration requires seeking out differences, valuing differing opinions, listening empathically and allowing for transfer of power.

How has collaboration served you well? What could you do to improve your collaboration? How does collaboration facilitate your success?

Jill Johns

JANUARY 13

Affirmation: *I consciously make empowering choices.*

Life is all about choice. You choose your values, thoughts, actions, attitudes, words, friends, associates, and how you spend your time. Even the things that you may think are obligations in your life are choices, such as getting up in the morning, feeding your children, going to work, paying your rent or mortgage, stopping at the stop sign or red light. These may seem obvious, yet they are all choices based on the values you hold and the norms that society dictates. Every situation, challenge, opportunity and decision presents you with choice. Whatever choice you make has consequences and either adds to your personal power, or diminishes your personal power. So, make your choices consciously.

Here are three questions I invite you to ask yourself when you are faced with making a choice. Asking yourself these three questions will support you in consciously creating what you want in your life.

How will I feel about myself when I have make this choice?
Will this choice enhance my relationship with myself?
Will I be walking my talk if I make this choice?

Whether the choice is a big or small, it is the consequences that count. Your "little" choices have a significant and cumulative impact over time. The power of a choice is whether or not it contributes to what you want to create, or whether it moves you away from that.

When you are clear on who you are, what you stand for and what you want to create in your life, your choices become clearer. You have the power to make your dreams and goals become your reality by the choices you make. Choose wisely. Choose powerfully.

Janet Christensen

JANUARY 14

Affirmation: *I choose what aligns for me.*

Do you sometimes feel like you are living someone else's version of your life? Are you busy, yet feeling unfulfilled? A full cup has no room for more water and the water will stagnate. To freshen the water, some first needs to be emptied out. So it is with your life. Consider reclaiming and refreshing your life by evaluating all that you do. Decide what aligns with your values and passions, then release those activities and people that have become stale and draining. You don't need to have it all; you only need what fits with who you are and want to be. When you release things that are superfluous and holding you back, your path becomes clearer and easier.

These questions for self-reflection will help you evaluate what aligns and what to release :

- What activities do I engage in because I "should" do them, or I don't enjoy?
- What things am I involved in that have become a burden or lost their appeal?
- Are there people/activities that sap my energy or are negative?
- What am I doing that is not contributing to creating the life I want?
- Do I feel like I'm in a rut?
- What could I release that would give me a feeling of huge relief?
- Am I fulfilled? Is something missing?

Take the time to reflect on where you are and where you want to be. If these are aligned, congratulations! If they are not aligned, what needs to change?

Give yourself permission to let go of chaos, energy drains, trying to be everything to everybody. Give yourself permission to live aligned with who you long to be, creating the life you desire.

Janet Christensen

JANUARY 15

Affirmation: *Today, I open to receive the goodness destined my way.*

Are you able to take in compliments gifted from others? Or do you quickly deflect and shrug them off? Are you open to receiving help? Or do you feel bad inconveniencing someone or think you should have been able to do it yourself?

Often, unconscious stories in our minds can block miracles and magic from entering our worlds. Stories like, "I shouldn't want more. I should be grateful for what I have. I don't deserve to receive. I'm not good enough."

The truth is, you do deserve; you are worthy. Your presence on this Earth makes that so. Open to receive the goodness destined your way. Embrace help and gifts from others so that they may fulfill their role on this Earth. Take these gifts into your body, heart and soul as gifts from the Divine. For around every corner, there is more abundance, more love, more magic and more miracles.

And your name is on them.

Paula Onysko

JANUARY 16

Affirmations: *"Go confidently in the direction of your dreams. Live the life you have imagined."* —Henry David Thoreau

The key to living the life of your dreams is to persistently take small steps toward your goals. Every small win you experience will build confidence, empowering you to take the next step toward your dream life. Before you know it you will have taken thousands of small steps and you'll be standing at the door of the life you imagined, preparing for a new, bigger dream to take shape.

Marcie Wingfield Shanks

JANUARY 17

"It doesn't matter who you are, or where you came from. The ability to triumph begins with you. Always." —Oprah Winfrey

Achieving small goals will motivate you to keep going.

There is so much you want to achieve. You know you can achieve each goal if you break it into smaller milestones. These smaller goals are stepping stones on the path to completing the large one, and *each step you take encourages you to move on to the next one.*

You always look ahead to what you can achieve in five year increments. Then, you set smaller targets for each year. When you take 100 small steps instead of one big step, you will feel yourself progressing, because you know it is just one small step at a time.

Self-acceptance is a work in progress and you can work towards this goal on a regular basis. Each morning, remind yourself to focus on accepting one thing about yourself.

Words of empowerment:

Today, I am confident that I can achieve anything I set my mind to. Each day is a chance to move one step closer to my goal.

Judith Duclot-Fletcher

JANUARY 18

Affirmation: *Nothing is impossible, the word itself says 'I'm possible'!*
—Audrey Hepburn

I truly believe that with God, nothing is impossible and all things are possible! I have witnessed unexplained miraculous recoveries in my practice as a nurse reiterating that "All things are possible." I have also had many strange seemingly "coincidences" in my own life. I know these "coincidences" were actually the "perfect coinciding" with the Divine. Whether simple coincidences such as thinking of someone and then they call or huge coincidences resulting in life transformations such as meeting the person of my dreams unexpectedly, I know these were Divine Interventions in my life. When my life felt impossible, that's when the possibilities arose.

We are all made in God's Divine Image. If we just let a glimpse of God's Divine Light shine through us, then nothing is impossible. Do you realize what a Divine gift you are? You are a unique expression of the Divine. You are here for a heroic Spiritual purpose. If you could see yourself as God sees you, you would never doubt yourself again! Marianne Williamson, in her book, "A Return to Love," describes this Divine connection beautifully. Nelson Mandela even used her excerpt in his Inaugural Speech.

Our deepest fear is not that we are inadequate.
Our deepest fear is that we are powerful beyond measure.
It is our light, not our darkness that most frightens us.
We ask ourselves, "Who am I to be brilliant, gorgeous,
talented, and fabulous?" Actually, who are you not to be?
You are a child of God.
Your playing small doesn't serve the world.
There's nothing enlightened about shrinking so that other people
won't feel insecure around you.
We were born to manifest the Glory of God within us.
It's not just in some of us; it's in everyone.
And as we let our own light shine, we consciously give other
people permission to do the same.
As we are liberated from our own fear,
our presence automatically liberates others.

Kim Evans

JANUARY 19

Affirmation: *"My time is now".*
—John Turner

Jessica had aspirations and dreams to move forward and because of life's challenges she was scared to step out of the box to pursue the desires of her heart. Jessica was always told that she would never be anything and this cruel statement caused her to become incarcerated by those thoughts. Jessica knew that in order for her to succeed in life she had to move forward in her thinking and nullify those words that caused a crippling effect in her life.

Now is the time for Jessica to press through her circumstances and to change her mindset. She realized that all things are possible and if she believed it she can achieve it.

Now is the time to declare over your life that *I can and I will have everything that is destined for my life.* Today is your day of change and you have just entered into a new season of new beginnings. Now is the time for you to walk into your divine purpose and embrace it. Now is the time to break through your glass ceiling in spite of your challenges. This is your day for your open door. Will you go through this door? I encourage you to go through the door because you will no longer live in defeat or captivity. Today is your day of victory and now is the time to break all barriers and move forward.

Donna Anderson

JANUARY 20

Affirmation: *"Any disaster you can survive is an improvement in your character, your stature, and your life".* —Joseph Campbell

When challenges arise in life, the first instinct many times is to ask "why me?" Next time a difficult situation arises, stop. Before reacting to the situation ask yourself, "What can I learn from this situation?" "How can I be a better, stronger person for it?" and "How is the best way to handle it?"

This will empower you to take control over the situation rather than becoming reactionary and possibly feeling defeated or overwhelmed.

When you view life as providing us with opportunities for growth and adventure, we gain control of the reigns and become stronger for it.

Remember that you always have control over how you react to a situation!

Maritza Rodriguez-Arseneau

JANUARY 21

Affirmation: *"If you love a flower, don't pick it up. Because if you pick it up, it dies and ceases to be what you love. So if you love a flower, let it be. Love is not about possession. Love is about appreciation."* —Osho

So many times in our life, we want to step in and "fix" people. We can see how they are broken and we can see how to put them back together. Oftentimes, in trying to "put them back together" we create more damage for them and for ourselves.

How can you stand at a distance, in observation of the ones you love, and admire them for who they are? Can you recognize that they are a perfect specimen? There is nothing broken or lacking that must be changed or improved upon. They are perfect in every way.

You, too, are perfect and require no "fixing." Regardless of what those around you may say, you are the embodiment of perfection. As the flower blooms and grows from its seed, you, too, will morph and change over the course of your life. One would never rush a flower to jump from seed to fully-bloomed blossom. Neither should one expect a human to make radical changes.

Stand back and appreciate the beauty of the flower before you. Appreciate and acknowledge it for you are in the presence of perfection. That perfection is to be cherished and nurtured, not cultivated or culled. Relinquish control for there is nothing to control. Nature is perfect and so are you.

Jill Johns in honor of Nicky Roberts

JANUARY 22

"It takes a lot of courage to release the familiar and seemingly secure to embrace the new. But there is no real security in what is no longer meaningful. There is more security in the adventurous and exciting, for in movement there is life and in change there is power." — Alan Cohen

Feel the energy in these words. While change can feel scary at times, it is more freeing than staying in what is no longer meaningful.

You are constantly being called to shed what no longer serves you. Whether that's clutter in your home, limiting beliefs in your mind, or draining relationships in your life, if it's not evolving you to a higher and richer place, then it is best to move it along. Clutter isn't bad. It simply reflects your growth. And you can create its exit without drama when you know that releasing is part of the growth process.

Start small. Release one thing, and then another. Then turn up the volume on courage for adventure and excitement. Courage is simply believing it is safe to take the next step. As you do, more information comes to you. Resources you didn't see before appear. Momemtum builds underneath your wings. And you become unstoppable.

Isn't that better than being stuck in security?

Paula Onysko

JANUARY 23

"The greatest weapon against stress is our ability to choose one thought over another." —William James

On the occasions during our lifetime when we find ourselves exposed to some life circumstances that leaves a doorway open for stress to make an entrance; quickly close that door then move to open a new door. Open one door after the other until you find the door that releases the built up pressure; I assure you that one of those doors will provide a gateway for you to escape. The choice to go through that door is yours to make.

Shirley A. Williams

JANUARY 24

"Don't waste your words on people who deserve your silence. Sometimes the most powerful thing you can say is nothing at all." —Mandy Hale

Conflict is the recruiter of those who are entertained by the sound of their own drama filled voices; however, your silence will send a powerful message. Your non response gives you the power and opportunity to remove yourself from their candidate pool.

Shirley A. Williams

JANUARY 25

Affirmation: *"It is one of the blessings of old friends that you can afford to be stupid with them"*. —Ralph Waldo Emerson

My friends are my brain's trust. In the moments when I cannot cope, when I do not want to go on, when I need someone to listen to my screams of frustration and anger, they are there for me. As I am there for them in those same moments.

They are also there when I need someone to enjoy life with, when I want to share amazing news, good fortune and great joy. They celebrate with me.

In the moments in between, we just are ourselves, in all our myriad of moods and emotions. We laugh over silly things, have catch phrases from movies we loved that we use over and over again until we happen upon a new catch phrase that suits our circumstances.

My friends have seen my worst, my best and my most stupid moments. And they still love me. I have seen all of theirs and I still love them. It is through the mirror of my friends that I find the richness of my life reflected and expanded upon.

Take this moment to appreciate the rich experiences that come through sharing your life's journey with the lovable, crazy, warm and giving friends that you have. Take the time to laugh over the little silly things, as well as sharing the large and amazing things that happen in your life.

Becky Paroz

JANUARY 26

Affirmation: *"Such is Life".* —Ned Kelly (attributed)

Ned Kelly is a famous Australian folklore hero. Whichever story you believe about Ned Kelly, there is no doubting the impact of his story on the psyche of the country. The accepted story goes, that upon being told of the time, date and manner of his death after his arrest, Ned Kelly replied, "Such is life". The simple acceptance of what had happened and how he was bought to that place is profound in those three little words.

I suffer from a debilitating disease – such is life. I have just received a promotion that I have been after for years – such is life. My best friend has breast cancer – such is life.

I care and I feel during these events, both pain and pleasure and occasionally both.

Both positive and negative events occur in every life. Having the acceptance that emotions come and go and, in any life event, that there is a mixture of both good and bad, gives you great power. Being able to accept that "such is life" gives you the ability to move through any life event knowing, that eventually, something else will come along, and present a whole new range of options and emotions. And I wouldn't have it any other way, would you?

Such is life.

Becky Paroz

JANUARY 27

"To thrive in life you need three bones. A wishbone. A backbone. And a funny bone." —Reba McEntire

Life has a tendency to oscillate between what we label "good" experiences and "bad" experiences. Sometimes we feel happiness, peace, and contentment and other times we feel sadness, despair, and frustration. What we imagine and dream of becomes our reality so wish for the things that will bring fulfillment to your heart, soul, and spirit.

One thing in life is certain -- things will change. Life requires clarity and flexibility. Adaptability ensures our survival, but we must also recognize the importance of taking a stand and having a backbone. Change is created when we take action on what we believe in. When we see injustice, we step up. When we see a problem we can assist with, we step in.

Approaching life with an eye for the quirky and humorous things that happen every day will make the trials and tribulations that occur in life a little easier to bear. Pets, children, and everyday circumstances present many opportunities to engage in the lighter side of life. Nowadays we have instant access to humor via internet sites, tablet applications, and email forwards. Take a little time each day to laugh and smile. It will lift your spirit, I promise.

Dr. Joanne Siebert, D.C.

JANUARY 28

Affirmation: *You might not be responsible for your heritage but you are responsible for the future.*

Choices are the door that opens up everything in your life. They give you power, liberty, prosperity and success. Your choice in life will decide your defeat or victory.

Cassandra Gaines

JANUARY 29

"Think like a queen. A queen is not afraid to fail. Failure is another steppingstone to greatness." —Oprah Winfrey

Today is Oprah Winfrey's 60ᵗʰ birthday. With a net worth of $2.8 billion, she is one of the wealthiest people on the face of the planet. I believe, for many, her name is synonymous with reaching and achieving big dreams. Thus, there are a myriad of reasons the world admires Oprah. But I'm most inspired by Oprah because of her boldness and ambition to be a high achiever and overcome the many challenges she's faced. These widely publicized chapters of her life include rape, scandal, abandonment, law suits and depression.

Many people are held back due to their victim mentality. They waste time feeling sorry for themselves, seeking sympathy for their hardships and blaming other people for their hardships. The reality is living through a difficult or traumatic experience isn't a unique human experience. Despite this, these "victims" share their hardship stories daily—much like a broken record—with everyone who will listen. Sound familiar? I suggest using the difficult experiences as a springboard for triumph and perseverance.

Inspire others to overcome the same challenges you've faced. Make the decision to rise above your difficulties and be the best version of you that you possibly can! Oprah did and so can you. It doesn't take wealth to accomplish this. Only heart and determination!

Dawn Jamison

JANUARY 30

"Goals give purpose. Purpose gives faith. Faith gives courage. Courage gives enthusiasm. Enthusiasm gives energy. Energy gives life. Life lifts you over the bar." —Bob Richards, Pole Vaulter

Our lives are a series of progressions. When a baby is becoming mobile, they develop strength by rolling, sitting, crawling, standing and then begin to take a few steps. Was their first attempt successful? As in your own life journey, it is a progressive and evolving.

Bob Richards eloquently shared his progression and he became the only two-time Olympic gold medal winner in the pole vault. The sequence is befitting for an Olympic athlete:

- Goals - objective/aspiration; write it down!
- Purpose - intention/resolution/determination; your destination
- Faith - assurance/conviction; believe it will come to pass
- Courage - bravery; in the face of odds to face your giants
- Enthusiasm - passion; like the Energizer Bunny
- Energy - power/vigor; the strength to endure
- Life - existence; voila!

Everything begins with a thought. First, you must conceive and shape it in your mind. The thought becomes a goal until realized. By writing down your goal/vision, you are 10 times more likely to achieve it.

To your success: goals, purpose, faith, courage, enthusiasm, energy, and life lifts you over the bar!

Lori Tsugawa Whaley

JANUARY 31

Affirmation: *"I do my best and remember that everyone, including me, always does."*

It is easy to fall into the trap of having high expectations and being hard on yourself and others, especially given the often frenzied quest for 'success'. Rather than berate yourself or criticize others for not living up to your expectations, remind yourself that you and others always do your best. Furthermore, your best today might not be your best ever, but that doesn't mean it's not your best right now.

Be compassionate with yourself and others; recognize that doing your best doesn't mean being the best... it means giving your best in any given moment.

Michelle Richardson

FEBRUARY 1

"Take care of your body. It's the only place you have to live."
—Jim Rohn (1930-2009) American Entrepreneur and Author

I don't know about you, but the older I get, the more my body seems to be breaking down and falling apart. My sister and I laugh a lot about when we turned forty. Out of the clear blue, we became allergic to certain things we had been around forever. Our knees, hips and other parts of us that never ached began to ache. It was if the universe had begun to conspire against us when we hit that blessed age.

The truth is that as we age we do begin to experience our bodies in different ways. These twinges remind us that we are no longer teenagers and that the sometimes senseless wear and tear we put on our bodies in the past might not have been such a great idea.

But now that we are wiser, and prayerfully more loving of ourselves and our continually growing bodies, we can really take a look at what it means to care for and love ourselves fully. Technology has placed us in a position to live at a fast pace mentally, but our bodies were not meant to move in the same way. Our bodies, no matter how young or old, say flow, take your time, and move in the spirit. Enjoy your temple, be gentle and kind so it will give you what you need to flow.

Kymberley Clemons-Jones

FEBRUARY 2

Affirmation: *"Go confidently in the direction of your dreams. Live the life you have imagined."* —Henry David Thoreau

Many of us are living the dreams of our parents, of our spouses or of society at large. We have been programmed to do things a certain way and that programming has come to us through other people. Our religion, our culture, and our education dictate our dreams. What would happen if you put everyone else's dreams down and picked up your own? Pause for a moment and think about what it is you truly want. What are your dreams?

Imagine for a moment that you have clarity on your dreams. What stops you from confidently chasing those dreams? What emotions do you feel (fear, intimidation or simply an incapability to pursue)? Think of what it must feel like not only to have dreams, but to confidently pursue them with abandon. Imagine the life you could lead, the experiences you could have, the fulfillment you would feel at the end of your life's journey if only you were willing to pursue your own dreams and not someone else's.

What if life events changed causing your dreams to change? What would you have to do to give yourself the freedom to alter the direction of your life? How could you change your dreams then confidently pursue them with a new-found purpose and confidence? How could you tune out the judgment of the world and stay focused on what is right for you?

I give you permission to pursue your dreams, with confidence. Don't be afraid. I won't judge you. After all, you deserve to have the life you have always imagined for yourself. Go ahead. Dream. Live.

Jill Johns

FEBRUARY 3

"Today I am empowered to follow through with my decisions."

Regular exercise and meditation practise have been proven to: reduce stress and anxiety, boost self-esteem, and improve sleep. But even with this awareness, maintaining a regular exercise and meditation routine can be a challenge.

To help you get started, realize first that 'trying' is not 'doing'! Don't start out by telling yourself that you will try to exercise and meditate two, three or four times per week. Instead - do it every day. Devote only 10, 15 or 20 minutes a day to begin with. This way you will break the habit of 'not doing' and replace it with 'doing'.

Second - no excuses. If you don't permit for excuses (e.g. too busy, too tired, not enough time) self-sabotage has no power over you!. Unless there is a valid reason (not an excuse), make the decision to exercise and meditate and, importantly, make that decision every day anew! This will allow you to stay in the present. By taking it one day at the time you will not become overwhelmed by your goal.

Gabriela Eikeland

FEBRUARY 4

Affirmation: *Intuition is your gift of wisdom; listen to it, believe in it for it is real.* —Barbara J. Bowes

Intuition has long been considered a "woman" thing and has never been well respected throughout the years of leadership research. However, once the concept of emotional intelligence was introduced, we are now seeing this philosophy begin to change. In fact, in my view, emotional intelligence is essentially intuition repackaged and sold again. So, if you've mistrusted your intuition up to this point, I ask that you rethink its value. Intuition is your wisdom speaking to you; it's your internal red flag that signals to pay more attention to an issue. Intuition is a culmination of your experience and sensitivity to the environment …it is your own internal means of alerting you to something important. Intuition is your gift. Make it work for you.

Barbara J. Bowes, FCHRP, CMC, CCP, M.Ed.

FEBRUARY 5

Affirmation: *"A good plan implemented today is better than a perfect plan implemented tomorrow."* —George Patton

I grew up listening to my dad tell me, "proper planning makes for perfect performance, and piss poor planning makes for piss poor performance." Although I agree that it is important to plan for your future, sometimes we can be paralyzed by needing the perfect plan to move forward. Do you struggle with needing everything to be "just right" before you can step out in faith toward new ventures, dreams, and goals? If so, you might be paralyzed by needing the perfect plan.

To overcome this fear of not having the perfect plan and being afraid of failing, make a good plan and get started. Remember that you will have made progress toward the life you desire regardless of whether you fail or not, sometimes it takes many failures to accomplish what we desire. If it's anything worth having it's worth working hard to accomplish.

Marcie Wingfield Shanks

FEBRUARY 6

Affirmation: *"Everything you want is just outside your comfort zone."*
—Robert Allen

As women we often find it difficult to get out of our own way, step out of our comfort zones and take a risk. We feel like we have so much to lose when we take risks, we hold so many placeholder roles (mother, daughter, wife, volunteer, boss, fundraiser, taxi driver) for others in our lives. Sometimes we forget to reach for the things we want, not just the things others in our lives require of us. The act of stepping out of our comfort zone creates fear that holds us back from feeling empowered and confident. What is just outside your comfort zone that you've been afraid to reach for lately? Is it merely taking time for yourself – to relax, to dream, to just be you? Whatever it is don't be afraid of getting a little out of your comfort zone. You'll find it's an exhilarating place to live.

Marcie Wingfield Shanks

FEBRUARY 7

Affirmation: *"People are like chocolate....sweet, delicious, light, dark, smooth, assorted, decadent and absolutely irresistible!"*
—Lori Tsugawa Whaley

Valentine's Day is a day for flowers, love, and most of all.... chocolates! When you open a box of assorted chocolates, the vast array is a feast for the eyes. People are like chocolates; we are all different kinds, sizes and looks.

Variety is the spice of life; imagine our world if we all acted, looked and dressed exactly alike and had the same name. How would we distinguish one person from another? It could be a real 'identity crisis' and paperwork/red tape could be a nightmare. Life would not be as exciting and fascinating. In relationships, opposites usually attract to make a person more complete. Different isn't bad....just different! If we are open, people that are different can bring out the best in us. As you find ways to appreciate differences, the differences will become more complimentary.

Forrest Gump said that 'life is like a box of chocolates.' I think that people are like a box of chocolates! The variety is limitless as are people! There is value and uniqueness in every person.

Take time to enjoy and appreciate the variety of people as you savor your box of chocolates! Irresistible!

Lori Tsugawa Whaley

FEBRUARY 8

Affirmation: *I get done everything I'm <u>meant</u> to get done today.*

What if you went about each day trusting that you got done everything that was meant to be done that day – nothing more, nothing less? Then everything that makes its way to a future to-do list is meant to happen in perfect timing on that day. Imagine how great that would feel. Imagine how the pressure would melt from your mind and body.

When we live life with this level of trust, we begin to flow with our tasks and to-do lists as opposed to pushing life. We open to a Higher Intelligence – a masterplan – that sees more of the picture than we can see right in front of us. Life becomes more enjoyable and peaceful, because our days flow from a place of ease and lightness.

Try it. Repeat these words. "I get done everything I'm meant to get done today – nothing more, nothing less." Then joyfully go about each task in your day breathing in this wisdom.

And everything that doesn't get done? Well, it's meant for another day. Voila!

Paula Onysko

FEBRUARY 9

There just isn't any pleasing some people. The trick is to stop trying.
—Robert Mitchum

I vividly recall my grandmother telling me, *"stand up for yourself and stop doing things to please people"*. Today, I realize how unwise it is to live life based on the mental thoughts of other people, whether verbalized or not. If you allow what people think about you to rule and reign in your life, you will not get much done; you would spend your life catering to other people, seeking to please them in every way rather than walking in your personal power and standing up for yourself.

No matter what positive thing you are striving to do; you can do it but you will not excel to your highest height if you are stuck with being consumed by what others will think of you or what you are doing. Do you find yourself asking, *"What would **they** think of me?"*

Be inspired to make decisions based on what you believe. Do not allow what someone else thinks of you to be a block to you living your best life.

Affirm: I will stand up for myself.

Frenetta Tate

FEBRUARY 10

Affirmation: *"Make space in your house for new energy.*
Get rid of the clutter!"

Do you save everything? Do you keep buying things you don't need? Are you bored and impulsive? We go through so many different stages in our life. Seasons change, kids leave from home, we start doing things we want to do in later life. What about your house, closet, make up? Is there clutter everywhere? Are you cleaning out and getting organized? It really feels good to get rid of things you don't use. Take your clutter to shelters or non-profit organizations that may be able to use it. Your junk is someone else's treasure. Start down sizing. Live more simply. You will actually notice the difference. I try to get my closet cleaned out, so when I get dressed everything in there is everything I love and I know that it fits. It makes getting ready a snap! Same with your make up, throw away your old mascara and foundation. It's really not healthy to keep old makeup. Plus, as you get older you want to simplify. You don't want your kids going through all your stuff if something happened to you. Don't give them that burden. Start when your kids leave for college. Every week do something to make your house less cluttered. This way it's not overwhelming. Try it! I promise it will feel like a good cleansing.

Angie Schultz

FEBRUARY 11

A part of kindness consists in loving people more than they deserve.
—Joseph Joubert

Love is in the air. Love helps us feel good. Love creates endorphins that lower our blood pressure and improve our mood. Our bodies and our minds like love. We watch love stories between animals and humans and feel kinder and calmer. We relish pictures of humans and animals kissing. Yet, we often forget that love is part of kindness that is not extended just to those in our family or want to be in our family, but to others who need a helping hand.

As you think about love, think about kindness toward those you love. In many cases we would do anything for those we love. Yet, we sometimes forget that **loving kindness also means forgiveness**. Forgiveness does not necessarily require the other person to accept your forgiveness. Certainly, you can tell them you forgive them, but even if they do not forgive you, forgiveness allows you to release negative feelings, thoughts, and emotions. It helps you become calmer and realize what is important. It allows you to love those in your life more. And when you love more, you are able to receive more love from others.

Practice forgiveness today. And, as you forgive another person, group, organization, your boss, commit a random act of kindness. Random acts of kindness demonstrate love. It will make you feel good, it will make the other person feel good. Even the act of smiling for just a few seconds raises our feel good endorphins that last for others. Smile today and practice random acts of kindness to demonstrate the love you have for life.

Katrina Everhart

FEBRUARY 12

Affirmation: *Never let the sun set on your anger. Seek peace with others.*

Let us remember the lessons learned on that fateful day of September 11, 2001. Indeed, the depth of sorrow within our country was beyond words. We suffered for lives lost and for families affected by this tragedy.

But a lesson to be learned from 9/11 is to understand that we have no guarantees of a tomorrow. Instead, no matter the anger you are feeling for a family member, tell them you love them before you retire for the night. You may not approve of their behavior and may indeed be justified in your anger, but tell them you love them. Those could be the last words they hear from you and perhaps the most important of all.

Linda Ellis Eastman

FEBRUARY 13

Love yourself first and everything else falls into line. You really have to love yourself to get anything done in this world. —Lucille Ball

As we ready ourselves to celebrate Valentine's, whether we have a special someone to celebrate with or not, remember to love yourself first. Loving yourself first, does not mean you buy yourself everything you want. Or eat anything you want. It means taking care of your mind, body, and soul. Loving yourself means at times, you will not eat that extra cookie because just 100 extra calories a day will mean you gain 10 pounds on average every year. Loving yourself also means appropriate exercise without making excuses.

Weight has a lot to do with how we feel, think, and even what we remember. Yes, some memory loss is due too much weight. Folks who are overweight are more likely to develop diabetes, high blood pressure, various forms of cancer, heart disease, as well as pulmonary embolism, polycystic ovarian syndrome, gastro-esophageal reflux disease, fatty liver disease, hernias, urinary incontinence, chronic renal failure, lymphedema, cellulitis, stroke, depression, osteoarthritis, gout, and gallbladder disease to name a few.

As you plan your Valentines, think about the best Valentine for yourself and **love yourself into a healthy mind, body, and soul**. Meditate for 11 minutes today whether you walk and repeat Sa Ta Na Ma with each step or you sit quietly in a chair or on the floor. Meditation has shown to help memory, reduce stress, and change your blood pressure and heart rate. By loving yourself, you will be able to get more done, even IF you add just one more thing into your schedule like meditation.

Katrina Everhart

FEBRUARY 14

Affirmation: *Speak your truths and confront conflict. Your heart will be much happier and healthier*

It's all about love and the heart. My son is a Valentine's baby. What a blessing he is. It's a very special day for me. Is your heart open? How would you know? Do you feel your heart connecting to someone else? Do you know how to communicate your thoughts and get out what you need to say? Are you afraid of conflict? A lot of times people who are afraid of conflict and don't speak their truth can actually have heart trouble. Do you know anyone like that? Getting out your emotional feelings helps to keep you healthy. It helps us to be authentic and real and vulnerable. Be fearless and learn how to deal with conflict, so your heart won't get hard. When you stuff your emotions it will eventually make you sick inside. Take care of yourself and know you deserve it. Only you know how to take care of yourself in a way that's good for you. Deal with conflict and say your TRUTH. It's very attractive and real. I promise you will feel so much better. Be an inspiration for yourself and others. This day is Valentine's Day. Remind yourself that its about love and coming from your heart. If you cant do something good for you, do something for someone else. You gotta have heart! Get in touch with your feelings.

Angie Schultz

FEBRUARY 15

Affirmation: *"I can handle all that comes before me"*

As a child, I loved reading Dr. Seuss because of the fun I had had with the rhyming lyrics and nonsense words. As a parent, I enjoyed sharing that same joy with my son. As an adult, I love the positive statements and motivation behind so many of the Dr. Seuss stories and sayings. A good example is the following:

> *"So be sure when you step, step with care and great tact.*
> *And remember that life's a great balancing act.*
> *And will you succeed? Yes!*
> *You will, indeed! 98 and ¾ percent guaranteed.*
> *Kid, you'll move mountains."* —Dr. Seuss, Oh the Places You'll Go

We often try to balance so much between career and family that it often does become a balancing act. In fact, many times we forget to add ourselves into the equation. But what does it mean to "step with care and great tact"?

While life may present many obstacles and pull us in many directions, it is important to stay focused and persevere. Then by remaining true to ourselves we can succeed. Follow this mantra and you will be amazed at the accomplishments you can achieve.

Judy Singleton

FEBRUARY 16

*"The most common way people give up their power is
by thinking they don't have any."* —Alice Walker

Adversity challenges you to think outside the box.

Enjoy the peace of mind that comes with smooth sailing. But you should also look forward to the opportunity to think creatively through adversity.

Adversity challenges you to do things differently. It challenges you to think in creative ways and from different perspectives. In most cases, this allows you to arrive at a tenable outcome. *You know that emotional adversity can come on when you least expect it.*

If a highly charged situation happens *it is important to remain composed when necessary.* Because of this priority, you should become creative in your responses to stress and challenges. You make every effort to allow positive reactions to shine through.

Recognize that reacting emotionally to adversity hardly ever allows a solution to present itself. Remain driven to resolve the situation first.

Words of empowerment:

Today, I accept that life sometimes throws curve balls and I am prepared for these challenges. I am encouraged by my brilliance and ability to create solutions.

Judith Duclot-Fletcher

FEBRUARY 17

Affirmation: *"I nurture the important relationships in my life."*

The quality of your relationships determines 80% of your happiness level. Why, then, is it so common to allow important relationships to take a back seat to things like work, time wasters, and urgent matters that are not important? Perhaps it is due to the assumption that these important people will be there once you've handled all of the other 'stuff'. Or, maybe you have an intention to make them a priority but you allow other things to get in the way. Whatever the reasons, it has a negative impact in your life.

Make time to nurture important relationships and put them first in both intention and action; by doing so you will be exponentially happier.

Michelle Richardson

FEBRUARY 18

Affirmation: *Put God first and you'll never be last.*

As believers we need to seek the word of God and always put Him first in EVERYTHING that we do. Once you get the concept and follow HIS direction, He will make sure that you will be the head and not the tail.

Cassandra Gaines

FEBRUARY 19

Today I take steps that only light my path,
remembering that as I light my path,
I light the way for others as well.

It's so easy to get caught up in the stories of my life. It's so easy to get caught up in the stories of the lives of everyone around me.

Am I living deep or shallow?

Am I remaining in the eye of the storms or am I tossed about with the waves?

Am I shining my light?

Am I a reflection?

A shadow?

Can I check in with myself? Can I pause in the moment? Can I stop right now and pray to 'lighten' up?

Yes, I can!

Sharon McWilliams

FEBRUARY 20

Affirmation: *"Peace begins with a smile. Let us always meet each other with smile, for the smile is the beginning of love."* —Mother Teresa

A smile is contagious, heartwarming, and is a sign of love and acceptance. A smile breaks the ice and could possibly be an invitation for connection, conversation and friendship. By smiling when you meet or greet someone, you are opening the door to future possibilities. It could also be the only positive emotion that person sees the entire day. A smile is a healing gift to both the giver and recipient.

It takes more muscles to frown than to smile; so why not smile? A positive expression on your face can reflect your emotions as well as influence emotions in others. A smile can make you and the recipient happier and healthier. If you act the way you desire to you feel by smiling, it can be the source of your personal joy. Rather than smile if you feel like it, you can be proactive, smile because your smile could warm another's soul.

Mother Teresa cared for and loved the poorest of poor; she was love personified. Her life is one to be admired and emulated; and most likely she greeted others with a smile!

Peace and love are gifts to humanity and it begins with a smile; let it begin with you!

Lori Tsugawa Whaley

FEBRUARY 21

*"Life has two rules; Number 1: Never quit! Number 2: Always remember rule Number 1. —*Duke Ellington

Near the completion of my first semester of undergraduate studies, I decided that I had to drop out of school because I was pregnant. However, before I could quit school, I had to speak with the Dean of Women. After sharing my desire to give up on my education due to my situation, she suggested that I speak with my professors to request permission to take exams. Although I had not returned to my classes for the reviews after the winter break, I managed to pass five of six courses. However, I was placed on academic probation. Yet, I realized that was better than failing. Therefore, I was glad that I had listened and followed the dean's advice. She would not let me quit.

Fortunately, a guidance counselor from my high school had stayed in contact with me. Whenever I missed a semester, he would always call me and ask, "Why aren't you in school?" Before I could give an excuse, he would say, "Let me call financial aid and find some money to get you back in school," and he always kept his word. Consequently, I was able to return to school each semester including the summers and earned the hours I needed to graduate. In addition, I was not on academic probation during that time, and I carried a "B" average during my final three semesters.

Giving up is never an option especially when you have people in your life who are truly concerned about your success.

Ann Ransom

FEBRUARY 22

Affirmation: *I communicate with authentic power, confidence and clarity.*

The words that you use have a significant impact on your self-perception, how you are perceived by others and the quality of your life. Be aware of the words you are using and consciously shift from using destructive and disempowering words to using powerful and empowering words.

Disempowering words	*Empowering words*
I can't (weak/no control)	I won't (choice)
I should (implies no choice/guilt)	I could (more powerful)
It's not my fault (helpless/victim)	I am totally responsible (ownership)
It's a problem (negativity)	It's an opportunity (open to growth)
Life's a struggle	Life's an adventure
I hope (victim/worry)	I know (confidence/power)
If only (whining)	Next time (learn from situation/choice)
What will I do? (whining/helpless)	I know I will handle it

Janet Christensen

FEBRUARY 23

I choose to see every situation as an opportunity for growth,
knowing there is wisdom waiting to be discovered.

So many times I can get caught up in the life moments of anxiety, of hurt, of anger, of sadness, of loss.

I may feel despair, loneliness, directionless, and separated from God.

I can't find my joy; my courage muscles have disappeared.

What if I choose to discover the pearl of wisdom in each of these life moments instead?

What if I choose to trust this moment to a higher power?

What if I choose to honor that time as a gift in disguise, a gift that honors my journey?

What if?

Sharon McWilliams

FEBRUARY 24

Affirmation: *"Everything can be taken from a man but one thing: the last of human freedoms - to choose one's attitude in any given set of circumstances, to choose one's own way"* —Viktor E. Frankl

Viktor Frankl was a psychiatrist who lived through the German occupation of his country and survived, despite being interred in concentration camps for most of World War 2. He wrote his famous book *"Man's Search for Meaning"* as a result of his learning in this environment.

He did not choose that life, it chose him through circumstance and timing. He knew he had one option to survive the horrors that many didn't – choice. His book describes in detail the difference between those who never gave up their choice to survive and those who gave into their circumstances. We cannot know the horror of that experience, and it is my hope that we, as a global community, never do again.

However, many people live everyday through their own personal hell – cancer, disability, abuse, neglect. These things still exist in our world.

When you have nothing left, when everything is stripped from you, then all you have left is choice. How you react to the circumstances that are thrust upon you is the only thing that you can truly own and call your own, no matter what circumstance you are in.

Choose right now, that no matter what happens to you, that you will never give up your right to choice who you will be and how you will be in any given circumstance. Choose to have the attitude of hope, grace, determination, belief – whatever it is – and let no one take it away from you.

Becky Paroz

FEBRUARY 25

Affirmation: *Whatever I gather evidence for, I shall find.*
I choose to become the detective for love and abundance.

Have you ever noticed that once one thing in your day goes badly, then the whole day seems off? Conversely, when you are on a roll with good things happening, they just seem to summersault into more goodness?

That's because you attract into your life whatever you are gathering evidence for. So if you proclaim you are having a bad day, the Universe will provide plenty of examples to prove you right.

On the other hand, if you intend for today to be amazing and go about gathering evidence of that truth, the Universe is more than happy to delight.

Your word is powerful. Set an intention before you get out of bed to direct the energy of your day. Make it specific, present tense and positive.

Example: "Today is amazing. I am blessed with gifts of love and abundance throughout my day."

Now go about looking only for the gifts of love and abundance. Ignore the rest. They are for someone else who has set a different intention. Did you see the love? Did you embrace the abundance? They are there, waiting to be found. Namaste.

Paula Onysko

FEBRUARY 26

Affirmation: *"If you think you can do a thing or think you can't do a thing, you're right."* —Henry Ford

High school baseball is as much a mental game as a physical one. The pressure players feel stepping up to the plate can be overwhelming. As the boys age, the pitches get faster and the stakes get higher. Girls come to watch the boys play. Parents look to get a return on their investment of time and money. Coaches and scouts analyze the talent.

The worst thing for my stepson is to face a curve-ball throwing left-handed pitcher. It's not that he can't hit a curve ball. And it's not that he can't hit off of a left-handed pitcher. It's that, in his mind, he can't hit a **curve ball** off a **left-handed** pitcher. And you know what? He's right! It has nothing to do with mechanics, skill or physical limitation. He's right because of his thoughts. He's right because he believes he's right.

In coaching, I spend time uncovering peoples' limiting beliefs. Beliefs that hold people back. Do you think you won't get a good job? You're right! Do you think you'll never find love again? You're right! Do you think you won't get a promotion? You're right! Whatever you think is true. The universe has a way of listening to you. Be careful what you think.

So far, I have been unsuccessful at changing my stepson's thoughts. No matter how much I challenge him to change his thoughts, he won't listen. Part of the problem is that he's a teenage boy. The other part of the problem is that he thinks that changing his thoughts won't make a difference. You know what? He's right! But what do you think?

Jill Johns

FEBRUARY 27

Affirmation: *Just for today, I will not compare myself to anyone else.*

Many women constantly compare themselves to others, and feel that they are just not 'good enough'. Look into the mirror and be thankful for what you have been given. You are equal to all other humans and have your own special talents and gifts.

Linda Ellis Eastman

FEBRUARY 28

Get Up, Dress Up, and Show Up!

When I was in high school, I was driven by a desire to succeed academically. I remember feeling different than many of my peers because on exam days I would get up early, do my hair and makeup, dress in my best outfit, and then head off to school. And I must say, I looked GOOD! Most of the other kids in class looked like they had just rolled out of bed, stayed in their pajamas, and never took a look in the mirror. Not me! Somehow I understood that when I invested the time to look my best, my confidence level rose significantly and I would perform better. Dressing up took away the distraction I would feel about how others saw me, especially since I didn't want to draw attention to myself for looking sloppy or disheveled. It cleared my head to focus on performance, not appearance.

The same effect happens to me today. I take the time to care for my appearance, even if I don't have appointments or if it's a day off. Looking good helps me feel good, which in turn has a positive effect on my performance. It's that simple! To strengthen our inner confidence, the best place to start is to enhance our outer appearance.

No matter what you face today, you'll be best prepared when you Get Up, Dress up, and Show Up!

Rebecca Sheperd

MARCH 1

*"We do not see things as **they** are, we see things as **we** are."*
—The Talmud Record of Rabbinic Discussions Pertaining to Jewish Law, Ethics, Customs and History.

We tend to believe that the way we perceive the world is the "right" way or the "only" way and that the way we see things is the way everyone else sees them or at least should see them. We believe that our truth is THE TRUTH. Unfortunately, this thought process is inaccurate even for the most rationally-minded folks out there.

The great part about us not seeing things as *they* are, but as *we* are, is that whenever we are plagued by negativity we can then choose to respond to the reality that we are seeing things from one perspective and one perspective only. Our perspective is one that has been built over the years from our own histories and experiences. This multi-perspective view offers us a challenge to either accept our perspective (which may be negative) for another, more positive choice!

Imagine what could happen if we could change our negative perceptions and thoughts for the better, even if it is a direct conflict with who we are and how we see things?

We have the power to change how we view things and how we respond in an instant! Isn't that wonderful news? When we are down and out, we have the choice to change our mood and our reactions to the issues, IN AN INSTANT! I don't know about you, but this gives me great hope in our future as individuals, family and world members.

Kymberley Clemons-Jones

MARCH 2

Affirmation: *"Today a reader, tomorrow a leader."* —Margaret Fuller

My mom is an avid reader and has always encouraged me to read. Books have been my constant companion thanks to my mom. At any point in time, I am usually reading a fiction novel, a business book and three to four magazines simultaneously.

I enjoy giving books and receiving books as gifts. Giving a book is like offering an adventure to the recipient. Receiving a book tells you a lot about the giver and the giver's perception of you. Books can be very personal and universal at the same time. Books can unite or divide.

The walls of my office are lined with all of the latest publications surrounding women in leadership, leadership in general and motivational publications.

Whenever I begin a coaching relationship, I always ask the question "Do you like to read?" If the client responds "yes," I am overjoyed. I know this will be the beginning of a great relationship. I gently recommend different books or articles that I feel are pertinent to their situation.

Reading opens the mind. Reading provides clarity. Reading stimulates curiosity.

Ralph Waldo Emerson once said "I cannot remember the books I've read any more than the meals I have eaten; even so, they have made me." In other words, "You are what you read."

Choose wisely. Choose well. Choose deliberately. You are what you read. I read books about leadership, entrepreneurship and self-awareness. What have you read lately? What have you learned? How has what you read made you a better leader?

Jill Johns

MARCH 3

"Today I take control of my stress."

Stress is a common physical response to events or situations that upset our equilibrium in some way and continuous exposure to stress can have harmful effects the body, mind and spirit.

Since stress can often go unnoticed for some time, it is important to learn how to identify when our stress levels are out of control.

An effective tool in helping you to do this is to keep a Stress Diary.

Make regular entries in your stress diary and record:
- The date and time of the entry
- The most recent stressful event you experienced
- The mood you are feeling

As with many things pertaining to personal growth and healing, awareness is the first stage in managing your stress. Your stress diary will provide for a great tool during your healing journey. It enables you to analyze your stress and take action on it.

Gabriela Eikeland

MARCH 4

Affirmation: *Come together with the love of your life.*

Are you getting married because you want your guy to rescue you? Does your guy make you look good? Are you going to be his lapel pin? Does he treat you the way you treat yourself? In other words, do you know how to love yourself? Do you value and honor you? Do you get red flags of things he does or doesn't do, and you just ignore it? Is he trying to minimize you to equalize? That means does he try to bring you down to make him feel better? The more whole you get, the more whole of a person you can create and find for you. Find a guy that you start out as friends with, and have fun. Hopefully you can communicate and have heart to heart talks. Have things in common you both like. Hopefully you are determined to find your passion and do what each of you love. Compatibility is great too. Don't get in a relationship where it's so comfortable where you get blindsided and you don't realize you are marrying a person just like your mom or dad. Example: say you are used to your moms abuse and now you are getting into an abusive relationship and don't even know it. Go to counseling six or eight times and talk it out before you take the big step. Do all you can to make sure you are making the right decision. You want to make it for life. Use your intuition and your gut, most of the time, it's right. When you meet someone and most of his characteristics aren't great, trust me he's not going to change after you get married. What you see is what you get and hopefully what you love about your new beau is that there will be more good things that you like about him then less. No one is perfect. Sometimes we don't get what we need when growing up, and never expect it from someone else. You need to first learn how to give it yourself and become more whole, healthy, independent, and fearless. You want support, positivity, communication, compassion, give and take, attraction, fun, happiness, someone who can make decisions, has passion for his work, and believes in a higher power. I believe your partner for life is out there. Experience life, date and have a lot of guy friends and really find out what the most important thing you want for you. Then you can attract the man of your dreams! Be fearless and true to yourself. But most of all be authentic and real. Being real is so attractive. Speak your truth.

Angie Schultz

MARCH 5

Affirmation: *"Throughout life people will make you mad, disrespect you, and treat you bad. Let God deal with the things they do because hate in your heart will consume you too."*

Sometimes we want to take things in our own hands. Some people just don't get it. There are givers and there are takers. Are you rescuing someone to feel better about you? Do you do things to keep your friends coming back because you're scared they wont call you? Are you the one always calling, texting and checking on your friends? Is it a one-way street? It really should be balanced. Start putting that attention you are giving you friend and put it on you. It may seem strange because a lot of us don't really know what it's like to care for ourselves. Forgive others; know that certain friends, one day, you will have to let go. You have changed and grown so let it go. Maybe when you drop the friends that are taking advantage of you and controlling you'll be able to focus more on yourself. We all change and seasons change. Get new friends that honor you the way you want to be honored. The more we become whole, the healthier we become, and the more healthy friends we create. Take a risk, take a chance, just be intuitive and make healthier friends. Nothing stays the same. Get an attitude and be good to yourself and pick great friends. Count your blessings.

Angie Schultz

MARCH 6

Affirmation: *I know what I need to do in this world.*
I will follow my passion.

We are all put on this earth for one thing, to give back and to help others. Of course we have to work on us being whole. We use failures and experiences to learn from. We create mirrors in our lives to look at ourselves (people are the mirrors). Finding our passion we get to live life in that creative mode. We are happy with ourselves and therefore want to share our earnings and inspiration with others. People that find their reason for being on this earth are just fun to be with. Love their enthusiasm. So contagious. True happiness is doing what you really love. Knowing that you control your own happiness, you can actually be happy all the time, even in the tough times! Keep your faith and fearlessness and know that there are many blessings out there for you. Do your best, try your hardest, be true to you, and take care of yourself. Learn what you like, find your identity, and shine your light for all to see. Be proud of your uniqueness. This is what people want to see. Be authentic, and not afraid to stand out. We are all waiting and watching. Be the front sled dog in everything! Go for the gusto!

Angie Schultz

MARCH 7

"Deal with yourself as an individual worthy of respect and make everyone else deal with you the same way." —Nikki Giovanni

R-e-s-p-e-c-t! Many of us grew up listening to what is now called "old school" music. Aretha Franklin spelled out what she was demanding, and back then I believe that a lot of us got the message. While she was commanding respect from her "man when he got home," the Staple Singers gave respect a different twist when they sang, "Respect yourself. Respect yourself. If you don't respect yourself, ain't nobody gonna give a good cahoots."

It is possible to respect yourself and to have others to respect you, too. First remember, "Not to think more highly of yourself than you ought to think." Next, "always treat others the way you wish to be treated."

Ann Ransom

MARCH 8

"Then one day, she decided to create a life she loved."

Decision. Each day, each moment, we get to make a decision about how we will live, how we will feel, how we will connect with others. When I lost my husband very suddenly in 2009, I remember thinking very clearly in the hours just after he passed: "Okay God. I know You have created me capable to handle what is happening, because You wouldn't place me in this position if You didn't." This was pure faith on my part, and I knew I had to make a decision in that moment how I would move forward. Did I really trust Him? Yes. Did I really believe He would take care of my young daughters and me? Yes. Through my faith and trust, I believed we would come out of this with more strength and fully resourced to move ahead.

Even more, I was overwhelmed with a conviction that we must still have a significant contribution to offer this world while we remain here. So on that day, I decided to start anew, to live out the life that God wanted for me, not the life I thought others expected to see me live. It hasn't been simple or too easy, nor always clear, what that life should look like. But in faith I know I am taking steps in the right direction. And is there any better decision we can make each day other than to trust in God's plan for our lives? He has always delivered on His promises. We simply need to take action. When we do, He takes care of the rest!

Rebecca Sheperd

MARCH 9

"If you have no confidence in self, you are twice defeated in the race of life. With confidence, you have won even before you have started."
—Marcus Garvey

Have you ever lacked confidence? What do you do when you think that you can't face a situation in your life? As I reflected upon my response to these questions, I recalled one Sunday morning during service when my pastor asked similar questions. His questions led up to an admission of his having gone through a series of obstacles in his own life. As I sat there listening to him preach, it was as if he had read my mind and realized the pain that I was going through. He surmised that when we are going through challenges, we sometimes lay down our "shield of faith." Furthermore, he told us that was what he felt had happened to him during a period when he was not able to explain what was going on in his life. I recognized that I could relate to what he said to my own experience.

Ephesians 6:13 admonishes, "Wherefore take unto you the whole armor of God that ye may be able to withstand in the evil day, and having done all, to stand."

Ann Ransom

MARCH 10

Affirmation: *"Be impeccable with your word. Speak with integrity. Say only what you mean. Avoid using the word to speak against yourself or to gossip about others. Use the power of your word in the direction of truth and love."*
—Miguel Angel Ruiz

My husband is a man of few words. I am quite the opposite. I often marvel at his restraint and at his level of concerned disengagement. He can sit back, observe a situation, construct his thoughts and then choose to keep those thoughts to himself. As I said, it is a strength at which I marvel.

When my husband chooses to speak, everyone listens. I assume that people listen out of shock, wonder and curiosity that this man who usually spends most of his time in silent contemplation is now sharing his thoughts with the world. When he does speak, he chooses his words wisely, not saying more than is needed, often saying less than we'd like to hear. After each conversation, we are left wanting more. That desire to hear more and to receive more of his invaluable insights is insatiable.

Unlike me, his tongue is not his weapon. He does not harm people with his words. He does not gossip or shout. Each word is carefully chosen. Each sentence is carefully crafted. Each verbal exchange is a true reflection of who he is.

My husband teaches me to put down my verbal weapon. He helps me realize that silence can be stronger than words. He shows me that each word carries its own burden and that I should choose my words wisely.

How do you spend your words? What impact do your words have on the world? Do you leave people wanting more or have they heard enough?

Jill Johns

MARCH 11

Celerity is never more admired than by the negligent. —Cleopatra

Celerity, or the swiftness of an action or motion, is important. Celerity is one way Cleopatra was able to keep her kingdom while others around her became Roman Territories under Roman Rule. Cleopatra became infamous while her male counterparts are just history. While women in Egypt, even before Cleopatra's reign, enjoyed more freedoms than women in the US have today in the 21st Century, men wrote Cleopatra's epitaph. Romans did not care for strong women, so they downgraded her abilities, skills, and accomplishments. To this day, a woman who takes the same actions is considered rude at best, while a man would be called strong and independent.

Celerity helped Cleopatra and it can help you. Actions are important. Decisions make a difference. We have to use information and cannot just take action without thinking or make decisions without information. Cleopatra used all sources of information. One reason why she was able to build armies is because she spoke nine different languages fluently. She actually spoke to the people. She knew everyone's concerns, not just what others said or what they might think. She went to the source and did her research. She did not wait for others; she did not feel ignorance was bliss.

While historians painted her as a woman who used sex to get what she wanted, she was well educated in math, science, chemistry, and religion. She talked with all sorts of individuals, and observed the actions of others. Think about Cleopatra's celerity and how you can use her example to make better decisions and become the commander in chief of your own life!

Katrina Everhart

MARCH 12

Affirmation: *I flow with inspired energy.*

You have likely heard how important it is to be 'motivated'. Did you know that motivation is always externally driven - by the expectations of others, circumstances or fears – and that it is always about achieving results? For example, some companies use quotas or a bonus structure intended to motivate their employees to produce results. You may feel obligated to perform duties because it's *expected* of you. You may act out of fear. You may need to solve a problem, like being in debt, or having health issues. Filing your annual tax return is an excellent example of being motivated to act – it is an *expectation* by the government with a due date and *consequences* of not doing it. Motivation can be hard work and, on its own, does not have a lot of positive, enduring energy.

Inspiration, however, comes from your spirit and passion, fueled by an inner drive. (The word *inspiration* comes from the Latin *in spiritus*, meaning 'in spirit'.) Inspiration is intuitive and provides a powerful flow of positive energy. You are *inspired* to express it and to take action. Inspiration allows you to respond to the circumstances and events of life with creativity and wisdom, and to live with confidence and ease.

When you are inspired, you inspire others. Your energy, enthusiasm and creativity make you a powerful role model. People are attracted to your energy and passion.

Inspiration gives you clarity about what you want to create and how you want to live. With this blueprint, you make conscious choices and decisions. You more effectively discern what **you** want from what other people *expect* of you, thereby honouring yourself and what is most important to you.

Janet Christensen

MARCH 13

My honour was not yielded but conquered merely. —Cleopatra

Cleopatra, Pharaoh of Egypt and one of the most powerful women in history, was also one of the richest, eloquent, well-spoken, and knowledgeable. It was not her feminine wiles that allowed her to rule a country and maintain its independence, but her knowledge and skills in management, strategy, conflict resolution, and negotiations. Certainly, she went to war, but only when she had to. By speaking nine different languages, she spoke directly to folks. She also knew the history and nuances of cultures and languages, not just her own.

The colloquial phrase, "pick your battles", quickly sums up her decision making. She did not just choose things she liked. She chose things that made a difference for the people who lived in her kingdom. She stored grain for years, and then when droughts dried up the food supply, she opened the Grain Storage bins to the people and fed them.

Using Cleopatra's example, pick your battles and know your facts. Ask questions such as - Does it make strategic sense? Is this for my edification only or does it help everyone? Don't use a pros and cons list to make detailed decisions, especially life changing decisions. Use an appropriate method with logic parameters such as a **Decision Tree analysis**. A decision tree makes you think about the different choices and which ones are most beneficial. Don't put off decisions; not making a decision is often like cancer. The problem gets bigger; the treatment options get fewer and more expensive.

Make decisions with facts, *not emotions, traditions, and pride*. Play devil's advocate with yourself and use the **Six Hats Thinking method** to find the negative, the positive, and weigh all the aspects, not just facts. Cleopatra kept her honor, even though outside forces, in the end, conquered her kingdom.

Katrina Everhart

MARCH 14

Affirmation: *Reach out and help another woman and stand by to reap the rewards.* —Barbara J. Bowes

March is International Women's History month; a celebration that started in 1908 and since 1977 has been recognized in Canada and the United States. It has now been recognized by the United Nations General Assembly. As women, we need to be cognizant that many of our sisters in developing countries are continuing to be faced with armed conflicts and philosophical prejudices that constantly throw their lives into chaos. They are being persecuted, harassed, raped, refused an education and, overall, they face unbelievable hardships.

At the same time, there are many women within our local midst who silently suffer because of a lack of resources, family support, education and finances. I, too, was once in this position. I left a bad marriage behind and arrived in a strange city with 2 children in tow, no job, no money, no family and no friends. A stranger reached out to me and helped me to find my way. Since then, I made a promise to reach out and help other women in need. I have been doing this for 25 years and am reaping the reward of seeing other women achieve, succeed and live happy lives.

Barbara J. Bowes, FCHRP, CMC, CCP, M.Ed.

MARCH 15

Affirmation: *"If you want others to be happy, practice compassion. If you want to be happy, practice compassion."* —Dalai Lama

When we recognize that most people are doing the best they can in life, we can choose to view them with a different perspective. This includes viewing our own self in the best light possible.

Be kind to others and especially yourself. We tend to be more critical and harsh with ourselves than with any other person.

Recognize that your actions and behaviors are often reactions to what is happening around you. I include how you think of yourself and the situation. By becoming increasingly aware of this, you can control your action and choose a kinder response.

Be kind to yourself and others by complimenting yourself and at least one other person today.

Maritza Rodriguez-Arseneau

MARCH 16

Affirmation: *"I am the architect of my future"*

As children, we often have very vivid imaginations. We have no problem with colossal dreams. As we grow older, we begin to develop self-imposed limitations that often affect our dreams. Simple visioning exercises can help us to imagine ourselves succeeding and reaching the goals we want to achieve.

By using visualization techniques we are able to mentally rehearse the steps needed to move to the next level. This process can also be very empowering. It can lead to positive feelings about ourselves and provide us with increased motivation to continue to move toward our goal.

Give it a try! Visualize where you want to be and then work yourself backward in how to get there. This will help you to determine the necessary steps needed to reach each milestone.

"The first step toward creating an improved future is developing the ability to envision it" —Unknown

Remember, the best way to envision achieving our dreams is by believing in ourselves.

Judy Singleton

MARCH 17

Hope is faith holding out its hand out in the dark. —George Iles

Rejoice in hope, be patient in tribulation, be constant in prayer.
—Romans 12:12

Once you choose, anything is possible. —Christopher Reeves.

As a young girl, I hoped for my own family one day, for loyal and faithful friends throughout my lifetime and a strong sense of achievement and accomplishment every day in whatever career I chose.

That hope extended to my ability to grow into a loving, kind and generous woman who was grateful every day for her life, her loves and her freedoms in all aspects of her life.

Waking up each day I am surrounded by my core and extended family, friends who are like family and the hope for my own personal family one day. The luck of starting a new business in 2011 and feeling a tremendous sense of success, personal and professional!

Looking at my life, I am loved, treasured and worried about on a daily basis. If it is not exactly like I pictured, then I have only to open up my mouth and speak the words of HOPE for it to change! My big sister, Lydia Ruth Kelsey Barnes, is a blazing example of hope for me to emulate as I get older!

Michele McLeskey

MARCH 18

"The privilege of a lifetime is to become who you truly are. " —C.G. Jung

Have you ever considered the life cycle of a butterfly?

The adult butterfly lays small clusters of eggs on a leaf. About a week later, the eggs "hatch" and a caterpillar is created. The caterpillar eats and eats and eats for its entire existence. Once it is done growing, it forms a chrysalis. Inside this secret world, change and transformation are occurring. Once the transformation is complete, a beautiful butterfly emerges. The length of time this process takes varies by species.

In some ways we are like that.

We begin as an egg, safely tucked away inside our mother's womb.

We emerge, hungry - physically, emotionally, and spiritually. Our existence is dedicated to devouring all that life has to offer. Whether it is food or information or experiences we crave, we consume and we transform throughout our lifetime.

Often the transformation is not visible because it is happening on the inside and the only person who knows it is the individual who is experiencing it.

But, at some point, the inner changes and transformations show on the outside of us and our true beauty is revealed for the entire world to see.

Allow the butterfly to remind you of your own ability to transform and become who you truly are.

Dr. Joanne Siebert, D.C.

MARCH 19

I am entitled to miracles. —A Course in Miracles

How long has it taken me to realize and internalize
that I really am a child of God?
When did I forget this?

How long does it take me to remember that bible verse,
'All that I have is Thine; the place on which Thou stand is holy ground'?

How long do I have?
Since I am entitled to miracles, as long as I need!

It's so simple.
All I have to do is ask, then get out of my own way to receive.

What a relief!
(Why do I have to complicate the Way?)

Sharon McWilliams

MARCH 20

"All of man's difficulties are caused by his inability to sit, quietly, in a room by himself." —Blaise Pascal

Do you know what today is? For starters, today is the spring Equinox, on this day in 1952 the U.S. ratified a peace treaty with Japan, it's also the death anniversary of Isaac Newton (1727), and the day Albert Einstein published his theory of relativity in 1916. All of these are worth mentioning, but still not the answer.

Today is the day I'm proclaiming as Spend Time with You Day! Today's the day to catch up with you! According to statistics, on average, 12.4 billion phone calls are made daily, and every day, we send 144 billion emails! So undoubtedly, we've found time to catch up with Aunt Nellie, Cousin Joe, friends and co-workers. We eat, text, Facebook and multi-task on the go around the clock. In this hustle-bustle society, you rarely take time to get in touch with the most important person of all — YOU!

When was the last time you've found a quiet place to sit and clear your head from the clutter of the day? No television, no phone, no kids and no computer. Take a moment today to do a pulse check and to get in touch with how you're feeling about life. Are you happy? Are you doing what you love? Do the people around you fuel your life with energy or are they are they draining you?

These are critical questions and exploring answers can improve your quality of life! Maybe it's time for you to cut back your work hours, trim down your social time. Maybe it's time for a vacation or perhaps you're overdue to start an exercise regimen. Don't spend another day neglecting you! Find at least five to 10 minutes today to meditate and listen to yourself. What are your body, mind and heart trying to tell you? Listen closely and find out!

Dawn Jamison

MARCH 21

Affirmation: *"My environments support me to be vibrant, energetic, and fully alive."*

Be it yourself, your body, relationships, physical spaces, mental, emotional, financial, nature or spiritual environments, opportunities abound to design them to fully support you to live your best life. When you become aware of the potential to positively impact your life through conscious application of environmental design, you open yourself to a deeper level of peace and fulfillment.

Mindfully choose who and what you will include in your life and ensure that they contribute to your vibrancy, energy, and passion for life.

Michelle Richardson

MARCH 22

I walk this day with Grace.
I tried to go it alone today without Grace.
What was I thinking?
Well, obviously I wasn't!
I need to put a sign on my forehead:
"GRACE---
Don't leave home without Her!"

Sharon McWilliams

MARCH 23

Affirmation: *"Give me a firm place to stand, and I will move the world".*
—Archimedes

Archimedes was discussing the theory of a fulcrum when he made this statement. He knew, that with the correct tipping point (fulcrum) and the right amount of force (a firm place to stand and quite possibly a lever), he could move anything.

The same principle applies when we need to move views, ideas, beliefs, structures that no longer serve us and our surrounds. If we stand firm, others must move around us. The more that stand firm, the greater the force applied. When we all stand firm together, we can move worlds.

Embed yourself in the rock of your conviction. Arm yourself with a lever crafted of your determination and your truth. Stand firm and refuse to give ground. The mountain doesn't get out of your way during a journey, does it?

Be a mountain in your beliefs, stand firm and strong, and you will move the world.

Becky Paroz

MARCH 24

"Courage is like a muscle. We strengthen it with use." —Ruth Gordon

Forgiveness restores Your peace of mind.
When you forgive others, you also liberate yourself from being weighed down by past events. You wipe the slate clean and start anew.

Forgiveness puts you back in control of your life. You focus on your own reactions rather than external events. Your resilience increases as you become more skillful at dealing with conflicts and disappointments.

Letting go of resentments reduces your anxiety. You know from experience that you commit many actions for which you need to be pardoned. *It is important to teach yourself that absolution is possible.*

Distinguishing between people and their actions helps us to protect our own welfare while turning the other cheek. Understand you can feel affection and concern for others without condoning behavior that contradicts my values.

Forgiveness becomes more automatic as we rejoice in the good feelings it brings.

Words of empowerment:
Today, I throw away grudges from the past. I enjoy the peace of mind that comes with extending forgiveness.

Judith Duclot-Fletcher

MARCH 25

Affirmations: *Self Esteem is to know your Dream* —Oprah Winfrey

Self Esteem stems from knowing who you are and not feeling intimidated. Being a dreamer is important to life's heartbeat; a hope, and image of who we are can only manifest through dreaming. Dreaming goes to the essence of our attitude, acceptances, approve and respect toward ourselves.

Cassandra Gaines

MARCH 26

"A bird sitting on a tree is never afraid of the branch breaking because her trust is not on the branch; but in her own wings." —Author Unknown

Have faith in yourself and trust in the choices you make. Let your heart guide you in the direction of what is right/comfortable for you and listen to your instincts when they instruct you to choose another tree. Self-confidence is motivated by what's in your heart and how you respond to your instincts. Look within yourself and find the wisdom to hear and follow both your own heart and instinct; shut down of all the other madness that can sometimes impact your choices by making you question the strength of your own wings.

Shirley A. Williams

MARCH 27

Affirmation: *Rather than waiting for the storm to pass…*
learn to dance in the rain.

There are many circumstances in life over which you have absolutely no control. Rather than letting life take you down deep into a well, learn to do the best with what you have been given.

No matter the obstacle or dark cloud, you can teach yourself to dance quite well in spite of it all.

Linda Ellis Eastman

MARCH 28

Affirmation: *"This too shall pass."* —Unknown

Have you ever found yourself in one of life's challenging moments, feeling like there is no way out? Maybe it's a bad boss, a sick child, or a relationship low point. These situations can feel frustrating, draining and seemingly endless. In moments like these, it is important to know that it is only a matter of time before the situation will change, moving you on to the next challenge. Everything in life moves forward, whether you want it to or not. Nothing stands still. Sometimes situations evolve quickly, other times they evolve more slowly. But always remember, that this too shall pass. Your child will get well, your relationship will improve, your boss (or you) will *eventually* move on. Head down, warrior! You can do it! This too shall pass.

This phrase is applicable during the good times as well. Whether it's your first day on the job, that phone call from a long-lost friend, or the laughter of your children, this too shall pass. Hold on to those moments. Cherish them. Acknowledge them. In times of joy and happiness it is important to remember that life moves forward, whether you want it to or not. There is no pause button on life so embrace each moment fully because soon enough that moment will pass and you will move on. If you can remember that time is fleeting and will pass sooner than expected, you can engage wholly and completely in the moment, seizing the opportunity fully as you will never have another like it again.

The good thing about life during challenging moments is that "this too shall pass." Don't forget to take time to enjoy the joyous moments as well because "this <u>too</u> shall pass."

Jill Johns

MARCH 29

If it is to be, it is up to me —William Johnsen

When you discover your purpose and decide to follow your dreams, you must not allow or engage in any conversations where you are being belittled or demeaned by anyone. You are smart enough, good enough and have the capacity to accomplish your dreams, reach your goals and make a positive difference in this world. My mother is a great example. She believed in herself and decided to fulfill her dream. She went back to college while in her 60s to study Information Systems and graduated summa cum laude!

You can be, do and have anything you choose if you hold the vision and put your positive action behind it to make it happen! You must believe in yourself, no matter what other people may say about you. You must remove the limitations and the labels that you are placing on yourself and reach for higher heights. Other people may attempt to place negative labels on you to define and limit you but you can rise above it.

Are you placing limitations on yourself? You have to be more determined to reach your goals than other people are at preventing you from getting to your destiny.

Be inspired with an attitude that declares, *"No matter what, I am going to fulfill my purpose!"*

Affirm: I am determined to reach my goals.

Frenetta Tate

MARCH 30

"What are you doing to make other people's lives better? Consider this every day when you wake up in the morning." —Dawn Jamison

Happy birthday, me! I thank God and my parents for the gift of life! It's always the day that I take time out to express gratitude for the blessings, lessons and growth that I've experienced over the past year. I even thank God for the losses because I believe that even those have purpose and make me stronger.

But more importantly, every year, I use my birthday to take inventory on my usefulness to my family, my community and this world. I ask: "What have I accomplished over the past year? How have I used my talents and resources to help other people?" These are a few of the questions that I ponder in hope that I've added value to the lives of those around me. This is the greatest gift that I can enjoy on my birthday— the reassurance of knowing that I've tried to make a difference in some small way.

I also take time to journal about my goals and aspirations for the upcoming year. I try to focus on the areas in which I need to grow and ways I can live a better life!

Most birthdays mark a day of gift-getting, partying and event planning. Although nothing's wrong with this, I challenge you to approach your birthday differently this year. As you celebrate another year, explore how you can shine a little bit of light in a dark place!

Dawn Jamison

MARCH 31

Affirmation: *I trust myself*

Every day we are faced with making decisions of varying degrees and intensity. If you are like many people, making decisions can be intimidating when you are afraid of making the wrong decision. This fear allows the voice of doubt in your head to speak up and may cause you not to trust yourself. Is there a way to step outside of the confusion and fear to be able to trust yourself to make the best decisions?

The following series of questions I find invaluable in making wise decisions. These were taught to me by Jonathan Kvarfordt, a gifted energy worker and musician who has helped me greatly.

Will this drain me? (If your answer is a 'yes', then go no further; if it is a 'no' proceed)

Will this overwhelm me? (If your answer is a 'yes', then go no further; if it is a 'no' proceed)

Will this produce energy for me? (If your answer is a 'no', then go no further; if it is a 'yes' proceed)

Do I really have time right now to do this justice? (If your answer is a 'no', then go no further; if it is a 'yes' proceed)

How do I feel about it? Am I at peace with it?

The goal with using these questions to evaluate opportunities and decisions, is to find those that resonate with you, and engage and excite you. You want to create a space that supports you in moving forward to be the person you want to be and do the things that truly inspire you. Trust yourself to make the choices that honour you, that are in the highest and best good and then hold true to your decision.

Janet Christensen

APRIL 1

"Breathe in, breathe out."

Yoga instructors everywhere

If you are like me and most people today, you have a problem breathing. Yes, I said breathing. It's so ironic that the very thing our bodies were meant to do with little or no assistance from anyone but God, is something we often do incorrectly.

Most of us hold our breath when we feel stressed or anxious, and if you are female it is even more probable, because we were often told to pull and hold in our abdomens so we could appear thinner. Yes, things have changed since the corsets of old, but not all that much.

I learned how to breathe correctly in a singing class and then again in a yoga class. It went against every fiber of my being to breathe correctly from the diaphragm, but when I did the world as I knew it began to change.

When you breathe like no one is looking at your baby pouch or muffin top, you feel rejuvenated! When our lungs fill completely, and our stomach expands, then our body and mind begin to relax and we are able to realize just how stressed we have really been. Take time today to breathe in and breathe out. Breathe in, breathe out. Breathe in.... breathe out. Now, don't you feel better already?

Kymberley Clemons-Jones

APRIL 2

Affirmation: *Education is the most powerful weapon which you can use to change the world.* —Nelson Mandela

April is typically the season where spring really begins to blossom, flowers and trees are "reborn" again creating a beautiful palate of colors. Everything smells fresh and for some reason we get more energy and generally feel more lively. It's a time when young people are busy preparing for graduation and reaching out to try a new summer job.

For me personally, April has been a celebration for the birth of my second son and it has always been a time of renewal when I think about what learning opportunities I can take advantage of. I start collecting books that I want to read during the summer vacation months. Education has helped me to succeed in life and to make a difference in the world. With my education I have taught English Second Language to immigrant children and families who fled war torn countries. I have been able to use my education to help other women succeed in their careers. Education has been a strong weapon for me and will continue to be a resource and tool the rest of my life.

Barbara J. Bowes, FCHRP, CMC, CCP, M.Ed.

APRIL 3

"Today I fully recognise that my inner worth has unlimited measure."

You have the ability and the wisdom to engage in practises that encourage a sense of self-worth and call for self-responsibility.

Your journey of discovering your inner worth and how to manifest it in daily life is truly an exciting journey of reclaiming your inner power. It provides for the inspiration to break free from limiting belief pattern and conditioning. It is a journey that brings forth the strength within!

Set the pace for this journey each day by embracing the capable and strong YOU!

Gabriela Eikeland

APRIL 4

Affirmation: *"Do not dwell in the past, do not dream of the future, concentrate the mind on the present moment."* —Buddha

I am a worrier. I worry about my kids. I worry about my husband. I worry about my job, my weight, my finances, my future. At times, my anxiety can become paralyzing.

I have also become very adept at beating myself up. The phrases "*I should have said this, I should have done that*" pepper my language on a daily basis.

In order to save myself from myself, I have selected a mantra to remind me of the Buddha's teaching. The mantra is "I am here. I am now." Whenever I feel the pangs of anxiety creeping in, I repeat this to myself as I breathe slowly and deliberately. Whenever I focus on the past and wish I had the power to change things, I repeat this mantra. This mantra brings me back to the present moment and reminds me that "I am here. I am now." I am not my past. I know nothing about my future. I am here. I am now.

My mantra is displayed on top of my computer monitor as a constant reminder to stay present.

What can you do/say to release yourself from your past? How can you avoid viewing the future with fear or despair?

If you can't think of your own mantra, feel free to use mine because these six little words, "I am here. I am now," have the power to change your life.

Jill Johns

APRIL 5

Affirmation: *"Whether you think you can, or you think you can't – you're right."* —Henry Ford

In the past several years there have been a considerable amount of studies done regarding the power of your thoughts. What has been discovered is: what you think about, you bring about. Everyone has fleeting thoughts about whether or not they can accomplish a goal, dream, or pursuit, but whether or not you dwell on it will determine your ability to achieve it. Focus your thoughts on your success and you will find success. Focus your thoughts on failure and you will fail. Sometimes you'll find the only positive thing to say about your endeavor is that today you are still dwelling on the goal. It might not always be going well, but telling yourself you can do it is half the battle. Your mind will determine your ability to succeed, so set you mind on the positive daily!

Marcie Wingfield Shanks

APRIL 6

Affirmation: *"I'm taking all the negatives in my life and turning them into a positive."* —Pit Bull

Absolutely! Why not? One way or the other, choose the positive. Life is made up of choices. Why not choose up and away! Be the eagle! Be all you can be. Find your best qualities. Ladies you know what they are! Appreciate what you have been and done in your life. We as mothers and wives wear many hats. We think that we can do it all. We just about do, but why? We can delegate and have people help us, it's okay. When we are strapped sometimes we need others to help us, just ask. Do something everyday you may be afraid to do. Set boundaries in your house for you, your children, and your husband. Teach your kids everyday in your most loving way. Tell your kids how important they are to you. Let them have their space to say what they need. No opinions given by you, just listen. Sometimes we need our kids to know that it's okay their own unique self. As moms we build the foundation in our family. Get them ready to spread their wings so we will be ready to spread ours. Be sure to let go so they will come back. No resistance. Let's be healthy moms for our children. Let's be an inspiration so they can be an inspiration for themselves. Be the example you want them to be. Have faith; your children already know what they need to know to fly high in the sky. Inspire!

Angie Schultz

APRIL 7

Affirmation: *Your past, your family, your life to this point is all for you to see, so you can make a choice for who you want to be.*

Are you an inspiration? Do you care? Is your attitude, "why me?" Do you want people to feel sorry for you? Is this how you get attention? Do you want negative attention? Are you needy? Insecure? Are you being like your mom or dad? Use your parent as an example of who you want to be. If your mom is a control freak, break the chain! Get healthy and whole and you can probably deal with her better, and even get along with her that much more. She did the best she could, and she didn't know any different. You know though. Change isn't easy, but not breaking the dysfunction on the family is even worse. Your talented, gifted, blessed, a child of the most-high G-d. You are unique. You have everything inside to be all of who you are. Take the risk be the inspiration in the family. You will not only be helping you, but you will be an inspiration for everyone to see. Trust me, the family will notice the change and it will give them the strength to be all of who they are. Be bold! Be brave! Test the waters! You've been elected to help make change in the family, so communication, understanding and compassion can be shown. Have leaps of faith that someone will notice, if they want to. Then they can see that change is good and the whole dynamic of the family can come back together as a unit. Be the mirror for that person to see themselves without telling them, but by being all that YOU can be.

Angie Schultz

APRIL 8

Affirmation: *"Most people don't listen to understand, they listen to reply. So true."*

Have you ever just wanted to get something off your chest and someone just keeps trying to force his or her opinion on you. Isn't it great when you can have your space to vent and the other person knows to just sit and listen? You get to vent with no judgment and get to feel better. You trust your friend to listen, and she doesn't make it about her. What a friend. I truly don't know any people like that. Everyone thinks they have the right answers and after all it's just an opinion. We all have an opinion, and it's just that! An opinion. There's really no right and wrong. Go with your intuition and be aware. You can sense and know what your friend wants if you just stay in the moment. Compassion could be a touch on the shoulder, just listening and looking at the person, and being concerned. Having good intentions. What a great gift you would be giving friends - the space to hear themselves. That's why we were given two ears and one mouth, to be a better listener and a backboard for people to express themselves. We could talk less and listen more. Awesome!

Angie Schultz

APRIL 9

Affirmation: *I radiate love and happiness every day*

There is a story about two dogs. Both of the dogs walk into the same room at different times. One dog comes out wagging its tail. The other dog comes out growling. A woman standing nearby witnessed this and was curious, so she went into the room to see what could make one dog so happy, and another so angry. To her surprise, the room was filled with mirrors. The happy dog found a room full of happy dogs looking back at him. The angry dog experienced only angry dogs in the room.

What you see in the world around you is a reflection of who you are. Choose to radiate love and happiness today and everyday and this will be reflected back to you.

Janet Christensen

APRIL 10

"There came a time when the risk to remain tight in the bud was more painful than the risk it took to blossom." —Anais Nin

Attract healthy relationships.

Healthy relationships are the only relationships you should permit in your life. Realize your life is better when you let go of relationships that negatively impact your life.

By attracting healthy relationships,
you make your life easier and more enjoyable.

Be a magnet for healthy relationships, and they will happen automatically for you. Quickly discard negative relationships and seek more positive interactions to take their place and do this joyfully and easily. Healthy relationships will make you feel more secure and at peace. You will have a more positive outlook on life when your relationships are healthy.

Words of empowerment:

Today, I choose to invite healthy relationships into my life and release those that are negative. I permit only positive people to come into my life and work their magic. I attract healthy relationships.

Judith Duclot-Fletcher

APRIL 11

I will not be triumphed over. —Cleopatra

Cleopatra lost her kingdom after 22 years of fighting outside forces. While marrying brothers and cousins was commonplace in the ruling families of Egypt, so was poisoning and murdering your brothers, sisters, and cousins who had different opinions. While illegal now in the 21st century, people still fight, some inappropriately. Spousal and child abuse, verbal and physical, unfortunately, have grown exponentially with the population. So has workplace bullying, road rage, and violence.

Cleopatra did not waver from her strength, but she did change her management practices and adapted to outside forces. At other times she fought back and went to war, strategically. She built armies and navies and was commander-in-chief while running the government and church. She survived numerous attempts on her life to become Queen of Egypt.

Cleopatra was clearly aware that **change is the only constant.** This is true today as well! <u>Changing does not mean you have been triumphed over.</u> **It means you are smart, and using your head.** Just because you adapt to change, it does not mean you have lost your will or have succumbed to others' will. There is no excuse for abuse, at home or at work. Beware of gossip, the passive aggressive form of bullying. It kills the spirit, damages reputations, and camaraderie between and among folks in all settings.

Change was the name of the game during Cleopatra's time, ie., 30 BCE. If change and adaptation was necessary then, <u>being old fashioned now in the 21st century is OUT</u>! Today, look around to see what is outdated. Have you heard others say you look the same? This is not really a compliment. If you have not changed your hair or makeup in the last year, it's time to change. Then, ask - what else needs to be changed?

Katrina Everhart

APRIL 12

Affirmation: *If you always feel the 'grass is greener' in someone else's, learn to fertilize your own lawn.*

Do you feel jealousy and envy often? Do you look at other women and wish you had their social status, fancy car, amazing wardrobe, or successful husband? Trust me, the grass is NOT greener on the other side.

You really cannot tell what is going on in another person's life just by looking at them. Rather than yearning for what others have, set goals for yourself and attain what is important to YOU. Let go of envy, jealousy and female competition. Compete only against yourself!

Linda Ellis Eastman

APRIL 13

Well-behaved women seldom make history! —Laurel Thatcher Ulrich

Cleopatra's legend abounds, we all know her name, but not what she looked like or how she dressed. She ruled Egypt for 21 years. The only likeness we have is her image on coins used during her reign approved by her. The one indication to her physical stature is that she entered the Egyptian palace when Caesar was in control of Egypt, rolled up in a carpet. Surprising Caesar when the carpet was unrolled in his presence garnered his favor. As an exile for months, she had made it past thousands of enemy troops who had orders to kill her. Her strategy won Caesar's favor and allowed her back into Egypt, her palace, home, and temple.

Cleopatra was educated like her brothers, in languages, math, science, and war. At 18, her father, Ptolemy died, and she became ruling queen with her younger brother. They were married shortly after inheriting the throne. Yet as husband and wife, as well as brother and sister and first cousins, the family tree was short. Marrying your own family shortened the family tree, lessening the number of rivals for the throne. It lent new features to the problems with sibling rivalry and family squabbles.

We recognize Caesar and Marc Antony, from historical movies, or Shakespearean plays, the general public knows Cleopatra. Cleopatra framed and strategized her own destiny. She built an army, a fleet, controlled currency, and dealt with street riots on a regular basis. We can be in awe of her accomplishments and think she is a one-time wonder; or we can learn vicariously from her example. Caesar knew the same struggles; Yet, he is history. Even though Cleopatra's history was written by men who disliked her and suggested she was not well behaved, Cleopatra is legend! Become your own legend! Don't become history.

Katrina Everhart

APRIL 14

Affirmation: *I approach life with Beginner's Mind.*

"The first problem for us all, men and women, is not to learn, but to unlearn." —Gloria Steinem

When we think that we must be experts, or to prove how much we know, we view things from the paradigm of our current knowledge, which can actually be limiting. History is full of instances where people were judged to be crazy because what they dreamed of did not fit the current knowledge and paradigms – the Wright Brothers and flight; Roger Banister running a mile in four minutes; the earth is flat; Thomas Edison and the light bulb – the list is endless.

The Zen Buddhist concept of Beginner's Mind, or Shoshin, invites us to let go of preconceptions and have an attitude of openness and eagerness in life. Beginner's Mind allows us to be open to everything, to all possibilities.

What would it be like to approach each experience in life this way?

- Would it energize you?
- Would it allow you to have respect, appreciation and gratitude in place of judgement?
- Would it open you to new ideas and solutions?
- Would everyone and everything become your teacher?
- How would that look different from your current mindset?
- What would you need to release, or let go of, in order to do that?

Today, you are invited to become a beginner again and enjoy playing with possibility.

"In the beginner's mind there are many possibilities, in the expert's mind there are few." —Shunryu Suzuki

Janet Christensen

APRIL 15

Affirmation: *"Forgiveness is the ultimate practice in self-care."*

Forgiveness is not about excusing the person or act that hurt you. Nor is it about letting the person off the hook.

Forgiveness is about relinquishing the negative bond that ties you to that person and/or behavior. That bond consumes your energy and keeps you tied in a cycle of negativity to include resentment, anger, guilt and/or sadness. Your thoughts often revolve around replaying the situation in your mind.

To free yourself of that mental and emotional bondage, forgive the person who hurt you. That allows you to regain control of your life. It gives you control of yourself and the direction of your choices. Be

Choose to forgive one person or behavior today and feel free.

Maritza Rodriguez-Arseneau

APRIL 16

Affirmation: *Whatever your mind thinks, your body will become.*

Let's face it! Your body is along for the 'ride' in life. If you dwell on poisonous, negative thoughts, in time your body will begin to react to this toxic Mind-Body connection.

Learn to be positive, even in the most challenging situations. Your mind can create chaos or it can create peace. Make the decision to create a healthy mental environment for your body.

Linda Ellis Eastman

APRIL 17

"It is easier to ask forgiveness than it is to get permission."
—U.S. Navy Rear Admiral (ret.) Grace Hopper

I consider myself a recovering people pleaser. I used to bend over backwards to make sure no one was inconvenienced and that everyone was happy. I didn't ever break "the rules." I walked on eggshells no matter where I was and who I was with, all the while keeping a smile on my face and making sure that everyone was okay. I thought if I was just nice enough, people would like me and I could avoid conflict.

What happened, however, was that I became resentful, angry, and just plain unhappy. I made my decisions based upon what other people thought and whether or not they gave me approval (permission) to take action on what I wanted.

Somewhere along my personal path of spiritual discovery, I came across the wisdom above and it quite literally, changed my life. I started taking appropriate actions using good judgment, but without having to consult anyone.

And guess what? No one said anything and nothing bad happened.

I realized that I was living in a self-imposed prison.

Be brave and start acting on your desires within legal, moral and ethical boundaries. Your world will expand and you will begin to feel the sense of freedom that comes from taking responsibility for your own decisions and your own actions.

And, you can always ask forgiveness if necessary.

Dr. Joanne Siebert, D.C.

APRIL 18

"The greatest joy is in giving; after all, God gave Christ for us."
—Ashley Ormon

As Christians around the world celebrate Good Friday today, we reflect on the greatest gift God ever gave—his son, Jesus. Although many people shift their minds to the suffering and brutality of the Crucifixion story and Christ's sacrifice, I challenge you to use Good Friday as a time to think about yourself! Yes, yourself. Take a moment to consider all of the opportunities that you have in the course of a week to give to other people. Now ask yourself, how often do you give?

Shouldn't we all use Jesus' death as a source of inspiration? Sadly, today's society is conditioned to look the other way when it comes to people in need or assume someone else will help them. But, what about us? We all can use this day as a call for greater social responsibility. We don't have to wait until the holiday season to give or help others. Let's face it, we all know people around us who could use help in one form or another. Maybe they need food, clothes, a ride, guidance, or financial support. Whatever it is, let's do more to open our eyes and hearts a little wider to do our part. And in your moment of hesitation, ask "What would Jesus do?"

Dawn Jamison

APRIL 19

The foundation stones for a balanced success are honesty, character, integrity, faith, love and loyalty. —Zig Ziglar

What makes a woman beautiful are her loyalty to and her friendships with other women, and her honesty with men. —Vanessa Marcil

I have been infinitely blessed with siblings more than the average family. I remember them in my prayers faithfully even if we don't speak for days, weeks, and months at a time!

My brother, Joel Davis Kelsey Jr., has been a wonderful example of loyalty. He has the same set of friends that he has had since grade, middle and/or high school. He is in his 50's today and that blows my mind! That is loyalty, long-term like family. They may not get together but once or twice a year (if that) but they remain in contact and true friends even today.

He works so hard to be a great friend and this is the loyalty to friendship that I see EVERY DAY. I pledge to be more like him in so many ways but in this trait. I want to go the extra mile in contacting my friends and commenting on their social media posts as I get older. I realize that my stepsister Constance Sue Pobst Johnston resembles this trait also. She has the same friends she made in college and remains in contact with them even today.

I didn't necessarily see this when I was younger but as I have aged I realize that life-like friendships needs to be active.

Michele McLeskey

APRIL 20

Affirmation: *"Courage is very important. Like a muscle, it is strengthened by use."* —Ruth Gordon

The analogy of courage like strengthening a muscle by use is befitting. As we age, our muscles become smaller and weaker due to physiology and inactivity. If we exercise and keep active, we can remain strong. Our bodies were meant to move, and exercise benefits both the mind and body. When we activate courage, we become more courageous.

The Samurai warrior trained daily even if there was no war; he exercised and was prepared to meet the challenge placed before him. They realized that physical exercise contributing to fulfilling his role as a Samurai warrior. The Samurai lived by a code of ethics and he would rather face death than dishonor his lord and the code of ethics.

Courage is being brave or valorous in the face of a challenge or danger, yet not withdrawing. Every day, you may face situations or challenges that require courage. It takes courage to live your heart's desire. It takes courage to tell your story. Every desire, dream and story is important and needs to come to fruition. As you take each step you take towards your goal, your courage will become stronger.

Like the Samurai warrior, with each step of courage, you will become stronger and more courageous!

Lori Tsugawa Whaley

APRIL 21

Affirmation: *Build your personal power by building up the power of others.*
—Barbara J. Bowes

Have you ever wondered how a person progressed so far in their career and how it was that they seem to have so many friends and such a large network of supporters? Their success hinged on the philosophy of building up the power of others. These individuals reached out to help others, they shared their success and they gave give the gift of friendship. Then, when help was needed, these friends in turn reciprocated with their help.

People who take the initiative to create loving and supportive relationships at all levels of their life including family, friend and the workplace are happier, healthier, more active and more positive in their outlook on life. They value the different talents that people bring to various challenges, they dedicate time to building and supporting their relationships and they listen with their heart and answer with their head. I consider these individuals to be the ideal leaders because they provide support, give freely of their time, encourage individual self esteem and work hard to make a connection with others. Instead of engaging in gossip, they look for ways to understand others and provide constructive and positive feedback to help people learn.

Building your personal power by building up the power of others is a strong strategy. Try it!

Barbara Bowes

APRIL 22

"Going green doesn't start with doing green acts—it starts with a shift in consciousness. This shift allows you to recognize that with every choice you make, you are voting either for or against the kind of world you wish to see."
—Ian Somerhalder

Dear Mother Earth,

Happy Earth Day! I'm writing to apologize on behalf of the 7 billion people on the planet. As if you haven't sent us enough warning signs through global warming and the increase in natural disasters, I'm saddened that we continue to live wastefully and recklessly.

In 2012 alone, there were 905 natural catastrophes worldwide, up from 820 the previous year. Just in the past several years, bottled water consumption has continued to exceed 200 billion liters annually. In the past few years, over 400 species of animals have been added to the threatened or endangered list, and carbon dioxide emissions continue to grow at an alarming rate (It was 391.3 parts per million in 2011 up from 388.56 in 2010).

What's most disturbing is in America alone, we throw away 210 million tons of waste every year. Two-thirds of our waste is edible and 42 percent of our garbage is made up of paper textiles. I hate to report that we are the only ones on our block who recycle. And I work at a large and internationally known organization that STILL doesn't recycle.

I know, I know! There are so many simple things that we can be doing to live greener. I, for one, am trying to shift people's behaviors. I've been very vocal about recruiting more green ambassadors. But this is a slow process. So please, have a little patience.

Thanks a lot,
Dawn

Dawn Jamison

APRIL 23

Music has always been an important element in my life. I fondly remember singing songs like "Moon River," "Autumn Leaves," and other classical songs of the 60's in junior high. Likewise, I am amazed that I still remember the words to many songs from so long ago. For this reason, I recognize that song lyrics can sometimes provide uplifting and uncomplicated messages about life and love. Thus, the lyrics to the Whitney Houston hit, "Greatest Love of All," say it all:

> *"I found the greatest love of all*
> *Inside of me*
> *The greatest love of all*
> *Is easy to achieve*
> *Learning to love yourself*
> *It is the greatest love of all."*

Ann Ransom

APRIL 24

Affirmation: *"Radiate your inner light...helping others find their way in the darkness."*

You must have a purpose.... a *'SPARK'* for life....this spark will start a flame which is your gift to the world. If you allow your spark to sit and smolder it will burn out but if you give it air to breathe you will see it grow into a beautiful glow of dancing flames! Let that flame travel within and around you wherever you go. If you cease to have your 'spark', those left in your trail will only see darkness and ashes. Don't be selfish....have a purpose.....live it with light so that you can bring the universe out of the darkness...one lost soul at a time. As long as there is truth and purity in your passion, you need not fear leaving your trailing flames.

Mary M. Romero

APRIL 25

Believe in your dreams and they may come true. Believe in yourself and they will come true. —Anonymous

What you believe about yourself will determine how far you will go in life.

What you believe about your purpose will be evident in the fervency of your efforts and the sincerity of your pursuits. It is about what you believe you can be, do and have. If you think you cannot, you cannot but if you believe you can, then you can and those very beliefs can open doors for you and raise you to the level of greatness you always knew was available to you.

My sister believed in herself and her ability to succeed. Her strong beliefs lead to her courageously resigning from a job of 20 years to become a prosperous entrepreneur doing what she loves. *It starts with what you believe.* It **does not matter what great things people say about you; if you do not believe it about yourself, it means absolutely nothing.**

What do you believe about yourself? You have got to have good positive beliefs about yourself so that negative labels will not stick on you.

Be inspired to believe great things about yourself deep in your heart.

Affirmation: *I believe in myself.*

Frenetta Tate

APRIL 26

Affirmation: *Limitations exits ONLY if you let them!*

Know you have no limits. Limitlessness is a state of mind. We are only restricted by our THOUGHTS!

Cassandra Gaines

APRIL 27

I focus on the Plans laid out for me by Love.

"The Lord will work out His plans for my life—
-for Your faithful love, O Lord, endures forever. —Psalm 138:8

Thank goodness that I can depend on Grace to help me follow that precious Plan.

Grace whispers, "FOCUS!"

Grade whispers, 'Hold on tight for the ride of your life!"

Grace smiles, "Don't worry. I'm here with you and for you all the way Home."

Whew!

I am devouring a big plate of gratitude here!

Sharon McWilliams

APRIL 28

"Love is after all a gift of oneself." —Jean Anouilh

Happy anniversary Mike Jamison! Today we celebrate two years of marriage and 20 years of friendship. It's a day that I reflect on our growth as a couple and my growth as wife. I didn't know what to expect at the beginning of this journey, but I love what we've built together.

The greatest lesson that marriage has taught me is how to continually give gifts to my husband. These are gifts of friendship, compassion, patience, encouragement, love, insightfulness, understanding, and vulnerability. Mike has taught me how to be a joyful giver, and he has taught me how to open my heart to receive these gifts as well. The very best thing about our marriage is that we learn from each other. Marriage has been a wonderful teacher and has showed me areas where I need to continue growing.

The adage is true, marriage is a give-and-take union, but nothing has been more gratifying than walking through life with a partner who loves unconditionally and enriches my life greatly. My marriage has helped me to set a higher standard in my life and examine all of my relationships. Are these relationships adding value to my life? Are they improving my quality of life? I'm thankful for a prosperous marriage. I'm thankful to be with someone who makes me better and I'm also thankful that marriage has taught me how to expect of great things from life.

Dawn Jamison

APRIL 29

"Even if you're on the right track, you'll get run over if you just sit there."
—Will Rogers

One afternoon while waiting for a bus, my friend Lynda and I decided to see about obtaining social security cards because we wanted to get jobs during our summer break. To our dismay, no one would hire us without any experience. As a result, we went to summer school instead. At the same time, I vowed that I would keep applying until I got an opportunity to obtain experience.

Finally, at age eighteen I got my first job as an enumerator which required me to go door to door to verify information for a city directory. At age nineteen, I had enough college credits to be hired as a substitute teaching.

Later, I got a job working in a doctor's office, scheduling surgeries, setting appointments, transcribing patient histories, and many other tasks. After that, one of my college professors recommended me for a job at a local radio station. Consequently, the confidence that I gained as news director helped me transition to a career in sales.

And as the saying goes, "the rest is history." However, for whatever reason I never thought that I was successful because I wasn't a lawyer or meteorologist like some of my classmates. That was until my friend, Joan, told me that she admired how I had always done the work I wanted to do and was never afraid to make a change. Furthermore, she explained that too many people have remained in positions that they sometimes hate due to fear of change.

Ann Ransom

APRIL 30

Affirmation: *"The world is waiting for you to unveil your unique gifts and talents. What are you waiting for?"* —Lori Tsugawa Whaley

There is brilliance, greatness and genius in you. People may have seen your gift and encouraged you, and for others, you may be a 'diamond in the rough' waiting to be discovered. No matter what your situation, you are absolutely important.

We need each other. If we were meant to live alone, we would all live on a private, self- sufficient island. Every one of us is here on planet Earth for a reason; for such a time as this.

Your responsibility is to bring forth your personal genius, brilliance and greatness. As you shine brightly, you are lighting the way for others to do the same. Dan Coppersmith wrote the following befitting poem:

I declare my brilliance
It won't be denied
The world cries out
For what I provide

I am blazing, amazing
I can't be contained
I am a glorious, fabulous
Radiant flame

I choose to exude
All this and much more
My wings are spread
Watch me soar!»

As you declare your brilliance and step into your greatness, realize that the world is waiting for you!

Lori Tsugawa Whaley

MAY 1

"In creating, the only hard thing is to begin." —James Russell Lowell

My coach is a wise woman. She turned me on to the phrase, "Eat the frog." I had not heard of this before but it has helped me tremendously since hearing it. What "Eat the frog" means in terms of my day to day routine is to get the things that are the hardest for me to do out of the way – first. Those anxiety-filled, cumbersome, and annoying tasks that I do not want do at all are the first things I do. For instance, it is sometimes difficult for me to make calls, especially to difficult people, so the challenge for me is to call that person first thing in the morning and to eat the frog first.

I have begun each day eating those frogs and in doing so I am freed to continue my day without reservations and plaguing thoughts of what I need to do, but really do not want to do. I am freed to be creative and productive the rest of the day because I have chewed and swallowed all of those disgusting frogs for the day. I am also doing something hard for many of us which is to just begin. Now go out and eat those frogs and create the world you desire!

Kymberley Clemons-Jones

MAY 2

Follow your passion.

You hear it in your head. You do, don't you? It's quiet at first, yet you can't help yourself but to move a little: maybe it starts with a little toe-tapping, maybe you move your shoulder ever so slightly to the beat. And then, ooh! You start to smile. Joy fills your soul when you hear it, sense it, feel it. It's the beat and sound of your calling, your passion, your soul's innermost desire. And it takes you by surprise sometimes, overcomes your disposition such that you can't help but show it to the world around you. It is contagious! Others feel your passion when they get around you. Others sense your purpose and focused direction. They are attracted to the positive energy you are putting out into the world. You are influencing them! In that moment you are taking the lead in your life, and empowering others to do the same.

Now wait! Before you let that go and come down from that moment of bliss, DO SOMETHING WITH IT. Go find your goal sheet. You know, the one collecting a little dust on the back shelf? Find it, read it, maybe even edit it. Then, DO one action RIGHT NOW that will advance you closer toward your passion…the very cause of the song in your head. It wants to be heard! It needs to be heard by the world around you. Don't let that go before you make a difference today!

Rebecca Sheperd

MAY 3

Affirmation: *Celebrate Derby Day!*

This is a great day. Derby day! Yes the date changes every year but it's always the first Saturday of every May, the greatest horse race in the world. This is about beautiful hats, fast horses, and beautiful women; a great tradition in Louisville, KY. If you've never been to derby, put it on your bucket list. There is so much energy and excitement in the air. The fashion is incredible. People from all over the world come to this event. They plan their outfits, hotels, their months, hats, and parties months in advance. It's truly an experience. That day of fun and excitement is a way to feel what its like to be and feel that way every day. Take off the hat, the pretty dress, and know you have everything inside to keep that confidence and great attitude. It's kind of a test to show you what you are made of.

Go inside and find that person you are and continue to feel like the women who got dressed, and stood out and shined their light at Derby. Step out of the box every day. Challenge yourself everyday to something you might be afraid of. Continue to be the best you can be everyday. If you can't do it for you do it for your kids. Push yourself to go inside and push yourself to be an inspiration. Count your blessings and be grateful for all you have. Live in the moment!

Angie Schultz

MAY 4

Affirmation: *"Today I have the strength to define myself by my own standards."*

What is it that is taking place within us when there is a consistent hunger for acceptance and approval?

In essence; negative self-talk! We are buying into the self-inflicted or learned notion that we are not good enough and that we must define ourselves by what other people think and expect of us. These beliefs into fabricated statements about ourselves deprive us of the ability to connect with our true authentic self.

Take conscious effort and pay attention to your thoughts and when they are happening, and then make the decision to not buy into this form of self-sabotage. Understand those thoughts for what they are; fear based fabrications that do not belong to you! Believe in yourself and move forward.

Gabriela Eikeland

MAY 5

"Grace strikes us when we are in great pain and restlessness…. Sometimes at that moment a wave of light breaks into our darkness and it is as though a voice were saying: "You are accepted." —Paul Johannes Tillich

I am a mother. I am a grandmother. I am a daughter. I am a sister. I am an aunt. I am a cousin. I am a friend. I am a citizen. I am a neighbor. I am…. Regardless of our roles at any given moment in life, we seek, we desire, we crave, we anticipate, and we want acceptance. However, in the grand scheme of things, we realize that not everyone, including our family, will always "like" us for whatever reason. When, if, and should that ever happens, we must remember "whose" we are even when others do not accept us for "who" we are.

Over twenty years ago I met a lady, named Mrs. Grandy, during a revival at her church. We exchanged phone numbers, and she became a mentor to me. Whenever I was going through a problem, I would call her for advice. One thing I had to remember when I called was to always have my Bible open and ready to turn to the scriptures she would give me to read. She always shared 1 Peter 5:6-7; she gave me words of encouragement, and she always told me to remember "who's" I was.

Ann Ransom

MAY 6

Affirmation: *"After all those years as a woman hearing 'not thin enough, not pretty enough, not smart enough, not this enough, not that enough,' almost overnight I woke up one morning and thought, 'I'm enough.'"*
—Anna Quindlen

Gremlins are that little voice inside your head saying "you can't do that, you're not smart enough, good enough, pretty enough."

"Don" is my "not good enough" gremlin. Don reminds me that I am too young, too girly, and too kind to be successful.

I met Don when I was 14 years-old. An older boy told me that I was not good enough. I believed him.

Don helped me apply to college: "You'll never get in to ND… you're not good enough."

Don moved to France with me: "You're not good enough to successfully live in another country."

Don didn't think I was good enough for management, for parenthood and for entrepreneurship.

Don is my friend…he is trying to protect me from failure. He doesn't want me to experience pain. Don is doing his job very well. I respect him and am learning to appreciate his perspective.

Today, I invite Don to the conversation and ask for his opinion. He tells me his version of the truth. He shows me how I may fail. He shows me the potential pitfalls. He points out my past failures. I listen to Don then I form my own opinion. Sometimes he is right. Other times I decide that I <u>am</u> good enough and I pursue my dreams with abandon.

Meet your own gremlin. Name him/her. Recognize when your gremlin shows up and think about why he/she has appeared. Honor that reason then think for yourself. Make solid decisions based on what you think is right, not what your gremlin thinks.

Jill Johns

MAY 7

Affirmation: *"We would accomplish many more things if we did not think of them as impossible."* —Vince Lombardi

Let's examine Webster's definition of impossible: not capable of being done, or happening. As you look back on your life, what did you accomplish against all odds? If you only listened to the doubters and naysayers, where would you be today? The human potential is far greater than we can fathom

A young girl named Heather lost her hearing at a young age due to a prescribed antibiotic. It took her six years to pronounce her name; how many people would have given up? Ballet was Heather's form of expression and she 'heard' the music through vibrations. She entered over sixty beauty pageant contests until she was crowned the 1995 Miss America. Heather Whitestone was the first Miss America with a disability.

Heather has always believed that the biggest handicap is negative thinking and people handicap themselves by concentrating on the negative instead of the positive. She does not believe in the word impossible! What impossible dream or task will you prove possible? With determination like Heather Whitestone, you too can accomplish your dream.

Think of the word I M P O S S I B L E as I M P O S S I B LE!

Lori Tsugawa Whaley

MAY 8

"You gain strength, courage and confidence by every experience in which you really stop to look fear in the face.... You must do the thing you cannot do."
—Eleanor Roosevelt

After three very agonizing years, I was able to finish the requirements to finally obtain my degree which would enable me to teach. In addition, I was even blessed to get a job before my graduation. However, I never would have believed that something I had wanted for so long could end so quickly.

The principal made a comment during a faculty meeting about work and one's responsibility to one's family. For whatever reason, in my spirit, I felt that the message was for me. Consequently, a few weeks later I would understand why.

My dad was diagnosed with early dementia/Alzheimer and some other ailments. After spending two weeks in the hospital, he was moved to a nursing home. At the same time, I had a brother with special needs at home and another brother in a nursing home to care for. I had no idea what I was going to do, but I wanted and needed my job. Yet, on the other hand, my family needed me. Therefore, after a lot of crying, praying, and stressing, I made the decision to resign from a job that I have wanted all of my life.

There are three things I have realized during these trying times: Firstly "The Lord is my Shepherd and I shall not want." Secondly, "Delight thyself also in the Lord and he shall give thee the desires of thine heart." Thirdly, "But my God shall supply all your need according to his riches in glory by Christ Jesus."

Ann Ransom

MAY 9

Affirmation: *"If we listened to our intellect, we'd never have a love affair. We'd never have a friendship. We'd never go into business, because we'd be cynical. Well, that's nonsense. You've got to jump off cliffs all the time and build your wings on the way down."* —Ray Bradbury

I call it "analysis paralysis". When your head gets involved in emotional decisions, like falling in love, that have no basis in rational, logical thought, you can get stuck and never make the next move. Fear freezes you. Your brain tries to protect you from hurt, which is good when you are about to burn yourself on a flame, not so good when you are about to throw yourself on the altar of love, or into the foundations of business building.

Emotions come and go, and that includes pain. It is a natural part of life, of the cycle of birth, death, loss and gain. Child birth is excruciating, so I have been told by my friends, but women keep having babies and creating the next generation of children. Most mothers think the pain was worth it when they hold their child in their arms for the first time.

Falling in love, starting a business venture, embracing a new friendship – they are all similar. They involve great daring and trust, the potential for pain, and the opportunity for great excitement and sharing. Our fear of pain sometimes does not let us see all the benefits.

So take the leap, and build your wings on the way down, have faith that your heart will manage and like the muscle it is, grow stronger from the use. Don't lock it away in case one day, it might get hurt.

Let go, be daring, take a chance, start a business, fall over that cliff in love.

Becky Paroz

MAY 10

Affirmation: *"One of the greatest discoveries is that human beings can alter their lives by altering their attitudes of mind."* —William James (adapted)

Believe it or not, our thinking and personal attitude reflects our outlook on life and our attitude toward ourselves as well as our ability to achieve personal and professional success. One of the skills I've learned and use frequently is the power of "self talk". Self talk is a strategy whereby you create inner conversations with yourself and continuously feed positive statements into your mind.

When I was struggling through a tough divorce, I continued to repeat the statement, "I am going to be strong for my kids" and followed it up with the statement, "today is a great day, I am happy to be alive and well". Whenever I felt myself slipping and at any time of the day or night, I repeated this mantra. It worked and continues to work in fact, I am amazed at how self talk has helped me to reframe my life challenges; put a positive spin on issues arising and continue to put positive thoughts into my mind.

Barbara J.Bowes, FCHRP, CMC. CCP, M.Ed

MAY 11

In praising Antony, I have dispraised Caesar. —Cleopatra

Cleopatra, known for her knowledge and language skills in 9 different languages, knew when words hurt. Unlike the childish rhyme that says words cannot hurt; they do. **Words build and strengthen relationships, words tear down relationships and sometimes do irreparable harm.** We see this on the political front all the time. Folks use inflammatory words to invoke negative emotions in hopes to damage other's reputations, innovations, thoughts, and ideas. In many cases, the situation is just because one group of individuals does not want others to have the same thing. For many this is discrimination, to others it is alright because they feel superior.

Caesar felt superior to everyone. Even just kind words about one of the individuals that worked with him, Marc Antony, displeased Caesar. While said in 40 BCE, human nature has not changed today. There are folks that are jealous. Kind words about others upset and aggravate them. Yet, it is important to praise folks for what they do well. This does not mean right or perfect all the time.

Today, **think about the words you use and the tone**. While tone is important, the words themselves can calm a situation and can inflame other situations. Facial expressions can be important, but like tone, they are not as important as the words themselves. You can say something is garbage with a smile on your face and folks could be happy in one situation and devastated in another. You can say Merry Christmas to someone and offend them, when you meant it to be a happy, pleasant comment. Words do matter, Cleopatra knew this and she learned from her mistake. **Learn vicariously from Cleopatra and don't make her mistake; watch what you say to *others and about others*.** *Good could be bad, even if you meant well!*

Katrina Everhart

MAY 12

Courage is not living without fear. Courage is being scared to death and doing the right thing anyway. —Chae Richardson

Success is not FINAL, Failure is not FATAL, It is the courage to continue that counts. —Winston Churchill

I get up each day and I am the same person I was the day before, an introvert. I could happily stay at the house for days, I daresay weeks, at a time without going out. EXCEPT to buy more groceries like say Dr. Pepper. But then I will have a moment after a few days and remember that I have touched lives that people only told me about way after I made an impact in theirs so I put my shoes on and get ready to enter the world. I put one foot in front of the other and move with purpose, with confidence, with authority as this is who I am at the center of my heart.

I smile at everyone, no matter if they smile at me. I want to pass my courage along so that it will infect others who may need it for their day. My heart is heavy when I reflect upon the many people I have met along my life's way and I wish I had been Braver than I was.

Listening to the Sara Bareilles song, brave, I play it when I need inspiration. I speak words of inspiration to my soul, my siblings, my mother, my nieces and nephews, and friends if they want to hear them. I play the song for one niece in particular who has had a really bad year struggling through bullying, low self-esteem, and feelings of inadequacy. I want her to see her Aunt be brave as her example for tomorrow!

I am so very grateful to have a few good people in my life that have shared how meeting me, spending time with me and talking with me at length gave them the courage to rise to the occasion. I smile, a lot, on those days and remember how courageous my mother, Betty Sue Crews Kelsey McLeskey Brinkley McKinney, was when she changed her life during every traumatic period over her 78 years.

Michele McLeskey

MAY 13

I am a daughter of adventure. This means I never experience a dull moment and must be prepared for any eventuality. I never know when I may go up in an airplane and come down with a crash, or go motoring and climb a pole, or go off for a walk in the twilight and return all mussed up in an ambulance. That's my arc, as the astrologers would say. It's a good one, too, for a person who had rather make a snap-out than a fade-out of life.
—Molly Brown

Molly Tobin Brown, born in 1867 to an Irish Catholic family in Hannibal, Missouri, was poor but dreamed of being wealthy. Hannibal society in the 1860s and 70s experience wealth and hardship. Opulence abounded in Hannibal due to the railroad and river. Molly saw kindness and excess from the wealthy. Molly's sister, a servant in one of the Hannibal mansions, allowed her to clean up after parties. From her experiences, she dreamed of being wealthy. She became determined to marry a rich man.

Her dreams faded when she married James Joseph Brown, known as JJ, a poor, but self-educated man. She said,

I wanted a rich man, but I loved Jim Brown. I thought about how I wanted comfort for my father and how I had determined to stay single until a man presented himself who could give to the tired old man the things I longed for him. Jim was as poor as we were, and had no better chance in life. I struggled hard with myself in those days. I loved Jim, but he was poor. Finally, I decided that I'd be better off with a poor man whom I loved than with a wealthy one whose money had attracted me. So I married Jim Brown.

Yet, JJ achieved wealth and richness beyond anyone's expectations. Following our heart does not mean we have to give up our dreams. Use Molly Brown's example, and think about how you can achieve your dreams by following your heart and being active in your community.

Katrina Everhart

MAY 14

Affirmation: *"All our dreams can come true, if we have the courage to pursue them".* —Walt Disney

Bina is the mother of five children who works full time while attending a local community college part time. Bina has a dream to become a successful entrepreneur but the struggles of being a single parent and raising five children have become overwhelming for her. Bina often stands at the window and dreams of owning her own company and she says to herself how can I accomplish this dream that I have received and be successful at raising my children on my own.

Bina needed courage to move forward and accomplish her dream. She thought within herself why should I sit here and ponder over these thoughts because she realized this dream can be a reality if she has the courage to move forward.

Bina whose name means "Understanding, intelligence and wisdom" decided to move forward with what she envisioned and dreamed. Bina decided to put her plan into action while she decreed my struggle is over.

In order to be successful in life you cannot stay in the same place .We must take a leap of faith and do something that we have never done. In order to become great we must have tenacity to pursue, acquire knowledge and to press through our pain. The time is now to grow, produce and fulfill your dream. This is a great day because it is the day of manifestation because I have decided to maximize my potential. This is the day that I move forward.

Donna Anderson

MAY 15

Affirmation: *Only boring people get bored.* —Mimi Ellis

How often have you found yourself saying "Oh, I'm so bored"? Have your taken a trip with your children and heard them say, "Mom, this is like SO boring"? Hmmmm, I think there needs to be an attitude adjustment here.

Life is to be lived to the fullest degree. What has happened to imagination? There should be no reason to feel bored as YOU can create the degree of excitement you desire.

Listen to yourself talk. Are you a boring person? I doubt it. Omit the phrase "I'm so bored" from your vocabulary. Instead, consider the opposite "Oh, I'm so boring". I have faith that you are not. Create the life you want and don't stand in the wings waiting to be entertained. You have the mind and creativity to challenge yourself to move from boring to exciting!

Linda Ellis Eastman

MAY 16

Affirmation: *Everything in life is temporary*

Everything on earth is just temporary and that is why we need to live our lives to the fullest. Take nothing for granted. Anything that you want to do in life, just go it. Don't hold back and wish later you should have done it.

Cassandra Gaines

MAY 17

"Failure is success if we learn from it." —Malcolm S. Forbes

Everyone has experienced failure. Whether you lost a board game as a child or lost a business in bankruptcy, the feelings are unpleasant to say the least. They range from disappointment and anger to despair and depression.

However, choosing your response to failure is the key to moving forward and developing resiliency toward life. Staying stuck in "why me" or "it's not fair" cripples our creativity and prolongs the agony.

A wise mentor of mine once offered this perspective – our minds are like Google. The mind will give you information in response to the question you are asking.

When you ask "why me?" your mind offers you the evidence (real or not) that supports the question:

- You aren't smart enough
- You always make dumb decisions
- No one likes you
- You just aren't meant to do this

When you ask "what is the lesson here for me?" or "why is this (event, situation, relationship ending) the perfect thing to be happening to me right now?" your mind may give you:

- I didn't consider all the options and needed more information
- I trusted the wrong person and they let me down.
- I didn't listen to my intuition and as a result, things didn't work out.
- I was undercapitalized for this venture and I will know more next time.

The information that comes from a higher quality question helps you clarify your next steps and moves you forward on your journey toward success.

Never, never, never give up.

Adjust your course and continue because you will get there.

Dr. Joanne Siebert

MAY 18

Affirmation: *I take action now toward my goal.*

Have you ever watched a mother duck with her ducklings? When the mother duck wants to go somewhere, she starts walking then the baby ducks line up behind her and follow. She does not try to get all the ducklings in a row first. She sets off and, without fail, they line up and follow.

When people have a goal, they often want to have most of the details and a comprehensive plan in place before they take action. Wanting to have all the ducks in a row before starting is perfectionism in action. Being wedded to a detailed plan can actually work against you as being so focused on one way may prevent you from seeing other possibilities that arise.

While it is important to know where you are and what you want to create, like the mother duck, you do not have to have all your ducks in a row before you take action. Take the first couple of steps toward your goal, then be open and aware. The resources, opportunities and people you need to get you to where you want to go will show up, often in unexpected ways. They may show up disguised as problems. Rather than letting a problem stop or sidetrack you, approach it as an opportunity and seek ways that it can serve your purpose.

Taking the first couple of steps and being open allows you to be in flow and respond to what shows up. You will be surprised at how things emerge and how you create what you want more easily and quickly than you had imagined possible. Be like the mother duck - take those first steps and trust that everything you need will show up.

Janet Christensen

MAY 19

Affirmation: *"I take steps daily to nourish my soul."*

Self-Care is one of the most important, yet often neglected, practices in life. In order that you may have optimal health and well-being, it is important to dedicate yourself to taking very good care of yourself. Whether that involves getting enough rest, having adequate 'down-time', taking time for yourself, nurturing yourself, meditating, having fun, enjoying time with others, or some other means of 'filling your tank' is up to you to determine. In order for you to be at your best, it is important that you weave it into each day.

Start today by taking the most important step possible to answer the call of your soul.

Michelle Richardson

MAY 20

Affirmation: *"Have the courage to say no. Have the courage to face the truth. Do the right thing because it is right. These are the magic keys to living your life with integrity."* —W. Clement Stone

Courage, defined by Webster, is mental or moral strength to venture, persevere, and withstand danger, fear, or difficulty. The Samurai warrior lived by a code of ethics; courage was one of the seven principles. Although the Samurai warrior is no longer in existence, their spirit lives on.

A modern-day Samurai warrior, Chiune Sugihara, was born on January 1, 1900. He was influenced by his mother of Samurai blood who shared her love of art, language and compassion for people. Being a bright student, Chiune›s father wanted him to become a doctor and take the exam for medical school. He took the exam but only wrote his name; purposely failing the test. It took tremendous courage to defy his father›s wishes to pursue his own path, especially in the Japanese culture.

Chiune financed his own higher education and was gifted in languages. He eventually became the Japanese Consul to Lithuania during the late 1930›s. Many Polish and Lithuanian Jewish people came to his office begging for exit visas to avoid annihilation.

He was faced with a crucial decision; did he obey the governments of Lithuania and Japan or did he follow his conscience and write exit visas? In Chiune's words: "I have to obey God rather than obey my government. There is nothing wrong in saving many people's lives…and because of this reason, I went ahead with redoubled courage."

Because of Chiune Sugihara's courage, in short period approximately 2,000 visas were written saving over 6,000 lives. Today there are over 100,000 'Sugihara' survivors. Chiune Sugihara was named 'Righteous Among the Nations' and is honored at the Yad Vashem Holocaust Museum in Jerusalem, Israel.

Remember, when you do the right thing, success it will bring.

Lori Tsugawa Whaley

MAY 21

I give myself permission to leap into the unknown!

Sometimes I take those small steps that are safe and seem to slide right into home plate right on schedule according to plan.

But there are times, when the creatrix in me says, "Enough of the toe dipping already!"

And, I find my reply is to LEAP with both feet into those unknown moments, just flat out free-falling right into that grand place called Trust!

I do find myself smiling big time!

Well, most of the time!

Sharon McWilliams

MAY 22

Affirmation: *"Find something you're passionate about and keep tremendously interested in it."* —Julia Child

I used to apologize for leading. Whenever a situation presented itself, I always seemed to gravitate toward the leadership role whether it was leading a group of my peers through the unknown streets of Paris at 17 years old or participating in process improvement project teams. I never really wanted to lead, but I always did.

I used to resist leadership, shrugging it off, not knowing how to do it well and not welcoming the opportunity. No matter how hard I tried to resist, I kept finding myself in leadership roles. Once I got turned on to assessments like DiSC, Myers-Briggs, and Fascinate, I realized that I am hard-wired to lead. I was designed to take the lead. This thing called leadership that I have been struggling to resist my whole life is actually what I was designed to do. It's my life's purpose. And if it's my purpose, I might as well pursue it with gusto.

Ever since I've had this awakening, leadership has become my passion. I love it. I love leading others. I love leading myself. I love watching others step into a leadership roles and succeed. I read about leadership and talk about it incessantly. My 9 year old daughter even wrote an essay about how she admires me because of my passion for leadership.

I have learned to stop apologizing for my passion. What if Julia Child apologized for being passionate about French cooking?

What are you passionate about? How does your passion manifest itself on a daily basis?

Quit apologizing for your passion, embrace it and get out there and change the world!

Jill Johns

MAY 23

Affirmation: *It's not what you look at that matters, it's what you see.*
—Henry David Thoreau

Beauty is truly in the eyes of the beholder. When you look at someone of another race, what do you see? When you look at the physically or mentally challenged, are you judging them?

Indeed, you look at many people during the day, but what do you actually 'see'? What are your thoughts? Judgements? Are you critical of others if they are different than you?

Open your heart and mind.

Linda Ellis Eastman

MAY 24

Affirmation: *"You can never quit, winners never quit, and quitters never win"*. —Ted Turner

Joan was discouraged because of the obstacles that were in her way that hindered her from achievement and advancement on her job. Joan believed that she could obtain a promotion on her job but she was afraid to go through the barriers. Joan wanted to retreat and quit because of the sabotage in her office. The sabotage was so overwhelming that Joan almost left the company to pursue another career. Joan felt hopeless and lost because of the opposition on her job. Joan began to realize that if she quits that she would abort her purpose and her assignment. She knew that her opposition was just temporary and decided to strengthen herself while she was going through this process.

Opposition can weaken or strengthen you however you must decide which road you are going to take. During times of opposition we must stand firm, be strong and tenacious. Opposition is only temporary and I encourage you to stay focused and keep your mind on your goal. Do not be moved by what you see but be moved by what you believe because you have the strength to do what you are called to do. Do not quit arise and go forward because you will forfeit your destiny. Why would you quit when you can become successful. Stand firm, be strong because you are in pursuit of your destiny and your legacy awaits you

Donna Anderson

MAY 25

Affirmation: *"I will pull from my inner self for strength and courage."*

At some point in our lives, we will all experience some sort of a catastrophic event. Whether it is the death of a loved one, divorce, a natural disaster, unemployment, or a major illness – all are a natural part of life. Our ability to handle these events is totally dependent upon where we pull for strength to survive.

We all have the ability to survive, but surviving and thriving are two totally different concepts. How often do you pull from your inner self for strength and courage? If you have not done it lately, give it a try.

Ralph Waldo Emerson has written many famous works. One quote from him that I am particularly fond of is, *"What lies behind us and what lies ahead of us are tiny matters compared to what lies within us."* This statement is so true. The strength and power from within each of us is incredible. It is up to us to harness that power and bring it forward. Once we do that, we can use it for strength and courage as we experience the tough times associated with life.

Judy Singleton

MAY 26

Affirmation: *"Our beauty encompasses our whole self."*

During our youth, many of us were bombarded with an unrealistic ideal of beauty and/or complemented on our "good" behavior. The message many girls learned was that looks and the ability to conform and play by the rules are of supreme importance.

Many of us have never been mentored on how our beauty is a summation of our physical, emotional, mental aspects of ourselves. Have you ever met a person and initially thought they weren't very attractive. After interacting with them, your perspective changed and suddenly you felt they were actually beautiful. You reacted to their "true beauty" that comes from getting to know the multi- aspects of a person.

Make a written inventory today of your personal strengths and attributes. Include physical, emotional and mental characteristics. If you have difficulty thinking of some, ask a loved one or a friend to help you out.

Recognize the totality of your beauty and have it shine through you.

Maritza Rodriguez-Arseneau

MAY 27

"The secret to mastery in any field is to forever be a student."
—Martin Palmer

Every experience and encounter can open the door to learning as you are presented with such opportunities. My brother is always in a mode of learning. He believes that one should listen to all advice because you never know what you will learn. He views advice like the grocery store. If you need it, put it in your cart. If you do not, leave it on the shelf.

Growth is a part of life. It is beneficial to be a lifelong student because there is always something new for you to learn, improvements to make and processes that may need to be refined in your life. Just as there are breakthroughs in the field of medicine and advancements in technology; there can be breakthroughs in your life, advancements in your mental and emotional capacities.

Our expectation is that the field of medicine will continue to find cures, develop vaccines and introduce new technologies and best practices. So shall it be with you; as you evolve, you do well to expect more from yourself in the areas of learning, growth and development.

Be inspired to seek better methods and adopt effective ways of living as you strive to be your very best.

Affirmation: *I am a lifelong learner.*

Frenetta Tate

MAY 28

Affirmation: *Do not go where the path may lead, go instead to where there is no path and leave a trail.* —Ralph Waldo Emerson

Dare to be different and think outside the box.

Linda Ellis Eastman

MAY 29

"You may be disappointed if you fail, but you are doomed if you don't try."
—Beverly Sills

You deserve love and accept it into my life with open arms.

Everyone deserves to have love in their life, including you. The amount of love you receive is only limited by the amount of love you are willing to accept.

Are you open to receiving love?

You are strong enough to overcome any feelings of doubt or inadequacy so you can welcome love without reservations.

By loving yourself, you allow others to love you as well.

Accept yourself just the way you are and love the person you have become. You will occasionally make mistakes, but you are still deserving of love, attention, and respect. You are free of the belief that only perfect people should be loved.

Love will help you make it through tough times.

Affirmation: *Today, I choose to accept all the love directed my way.*
I remind myself that I deserve love and all the wonderful feelings associated with it.

Judith Duclot-Fletcher

MAY 30

Affirmation: *People are more likely to be happy at work if motivation comes from within.* —Maynard Brusman, psychologist

Have you ever been dissatisfied in your job? Were salary and benefits the problem? Was the actual work task the problem? No, more than likely you were not happy at work because the job did not satisfy your personal motivators. The other side of that problem is that many people do not understand just what their personal motivators are!

There are eight different personal motivators. Any job you take must satisfy at least three of your motivators or you will not be happy in their job. These motivators include such elements having independence and autonomy, utilizing specific technical and/or managerial expertise and feeling a sense of security, belonging and identity with the employer and/or their location. Still others are motivated by a sense of social service and just cause or they need to be continually stimulated by a challenge and/or an entrepreneurial environment. Others are motivated by a more structured environment where life work balance is a priority.

These motivators create an intrinsic, internal self motivated drive to succeed. Take time for learn what motivates you! Your overall success hinges on this knowledge.

Barbara J. Bowes, FCHRP, CMC, CCP, M.Ed

MAY 31

"It's not what you call me, but what I answer to." —African proverb

Your confidence is visible in your appearance.

Stand tall and broad with a positive, yet calm facial expression. Take your time getting ready for your day.

Your appearance is important to gaining respect from others and feeling good about yourself. Each day when you dress with your personal needs in mind, You positively influence those around you.

A careless appearance evokes a mediocre vibe, even though you know you deserve esteem.

When you are feeling less than grand, you allow your appearance to deflect your inner emotions.

Knowing my outer appearance is put together and neat allows my mind to become orderly and helps me push away any negative thoughts.

Approach your appearance with only positive thoughts. You know what your body looks like and what looks favorable on your body type. You know what colors make your eyes look outstanding and which shoes make you stand tall and proud.

The way you walk into a room, how you sit in a chair, and how you face another person when you greet them are all actions that others judge. Having a put together appearance and welcoming body language shows your true persona.

Your appearance is in your complete control. You have power of your appearance.

Affirmation: *Today, even though I dress to please myself, I also choose to dress to impress. My self-esteem is derived from my opinion of myself, but earning respect from others is important to me too.*

Judith Duclot-Fletcher

JUNE 1

"Freedom Is Not Free" —Retired U.S. Air Force Colonel, Walter Hitchcock, of New Mexico Military Institute

Humanity is always searching for happiness and joy and we believe that when we finally find that freedom we desire, we will no longer have any trials or tribulations. We equate being free with little or no responsibility. We think freedom is about flying high, soaring, the feeling of weightlessness and the absence of struggle and hardships, but I've discovered that freedom really isn't free and if there is something called "freedom" it comes with the price called struggle.

You hear of prisoners who feel free. Is it because life is so nice for them? Is it because they don't have to think through their day or that they don't have to commute to work or could it be that their minds are no longer under any illusion that freedom is supposed to be easy.

We will never be without struggle and, in fact, we should not pray to be void of struggle because the struggles we go through, day in and day out, are not hindering our freedom, rather these struggles are helping and leading us towards freedom. The struggle is what helps us grow and mature.

Struggle motivates us and inspires us to a new reality. So the next time you find yourself in a fight for your life, instead of trying to find the elusive freedom we are always searching for, recognize that the true freedom to be obtained comes only through struggle and the overcoming of our minds!

Kymberley Clemons-Jones

JUNE 2

Affirmation: *"I mindfully foster love, respect and greatness at home and at large."*

Greatness exists within you and everyone on the planet. You might not believe this right now, but it is true; the potential for greatness lies within each of us. The challenge and the opportunity are to own it, deliver it, and evoke it in others. By fostering loving, respectful, supportive relationships with ourselves and others, we allow our own greatness and that of others to shine through. By delivering the best of ourselves, we lead by example and open the door for others to deliver their best. Support and encourage others and evoke greatness in them.

Identify what is great about you (involve others in the process if necessary) and then set about to deliver on that greatness. The positive ripple effect that this will have in your world and the world is immeasurable.

Michelle Richardson

JUNE 3

"Today fear of success has no power."

Fear of success may mean something different for each woman. It could be that you don't think you deserve to be successful...or perhaps you believe that you might not have what it takes. Whatever your thoughts are, remember that those beliefs are not based on truth and on who you really are; there is no truth to negative self-talk!

Understanding this, will allow you to move to the next step; a key component in overcoming fear of success is to understand that if we refuse to recognise what life is trying to teach us about ourselves we can't move forward. True Self-knowledge is vital in order for us to reach our highest potential and truly understand and embrace what it means to be successful.

You are able and deserving! Go for it!

Gabriela Eikeland

JUNE 4

Affirmation: *I am the designer of my life.*

There is a saying that if you don't know where you are going, any path will do.

Every person creates results in their life, either by default or by design. Those who create results by default take what comes and settle for the circumstances that life gives them, for the most part. Those people who create results by design are deliberate thinkers and creators. They take personal responsibility for their lives, have clear intention, focused attention and take action.

You have the choice whether to live by default or by design. Whichever choice you make, you will spend your finite resources of time and energy creating your results. You are invited to embrace being the conscious designer of your life – that makes more effective use of your time and energy and is much more rewarding!

Janet Christensen

JUNE 5

Affirmation: *"I will associate with people who are consistent with the person I want to be."*

It is important that we look around at the people we associate with as they are often a reflection of who we become. My husband is not only my partner, he is my best friend. I look up to him and enjoy his company, but I also want to emulate him. He is well respected by his peers and has a great sense of humor. He works hard, has integrity, and is genuine. When times get tough, he is able to keep things light and makes me feel at ease.

"Surround yourself with people who provide you with support and love and remember to give back as much as you can in return." – Karen Kain. This quote is another example of why we need to look at those we associate with carefully. My husband is my biggest supporter in everything I do. He keeps me grounded and helps me to look at all situations objectively.

After 30 years of marriage, I can definitely say my husband has been a positive influence on me and my life. He has nurtured me yet allowed me to grow in my own direction. He has definitely been an inspiration for all I have personally achieved.

Look around—do you have the same type of people around you? Our partner, friends, and family can be a lifeline or an obstruction. Make sure you have the right type of associates around that will lift you up and move your forward. Those that push you back and hold you down need to be released and allowed to move on without you. The old saying of "choose your friends wisely" has a vast amount of value to it.

Judy Singleton

JUNE 6

Affirmation: *"A thief of possessions is a criminal indeed but, far more sinister, desperate and destructive is the thief of mind, body, soul, and spirit. Never give what someone would choose to steal."*

If you have ever been the victim of property theft or a home break-in, you know just how devastating this can be. Yet, if we consider the worth of material possessions as compared to our own self-worth, there is no comparison.

I think we have all met someone in our lives that seem to have the ability to drain all our energy by their mere presence. This individual seems to be able to suck the life force from your body with a forked tongue or mean spirited action. Do you know someone like this? Persons like these truly would like to steal the part of you that makes you 'you'! Never give away what someone wants to steal. In other words, always remember your self-worth and dignity. You are a special light in this world and deserve to shine without the thieves of this world who would like to douse your flame.

Remove the people from your life that only produce negativity for you. In this way, you will always have the freedom of your own mind, body, soul, and spirit. Do not let anyone steal your life force. Be like the perfect drop of rain that glistens like a diamond on its way down, not like the stagnant muddy puddle that simply waits to dissipate because, our lives are but a mere drop in the span of a lifetime. Will you go out like the diamond drop of rain or the muddy puddle? Shine On!

Mary M. Romero

JUNE 7

Affirmation: *"The best and most beautiful things in the world cannot be seen or even touched – they must be felt with the heart."* —Helen Keller

Born deaf, dumb and blind, Helen Keller learned to adapt to the world. Helen›s teacher/mentor, Anne Sullivan, introduced her to a world that had not previously existed. Eventually, Helen embraced her new life, paved the way and opened the world for future generations with disabilities. Her contributions are still affecting mankind.

In the middle of the night, there is no light or sound; it is a solitary place. Imagine Helen Keller›s world with no sight or sounds....for a lifetime. Yet, she believed the most beautiful things in the world were felt with the heart. Helen understood that the human heart connection was more meaningful than anything that could be seen or touched In life, do we place more emphasis on ‹things› than making heart connections?

The heart connection is a strong connection. As you hold a precious baby, hug a loved one or hold the frail hand of an elderly person, your heart connects with another heart. It is a beautiful thing. Time spent in heart connections is time well spent; time you will unlikely regret.

Remember that the best things in life cannot be touched but can be felt with the heart.

Lori Tsugawa Whaley

JUNE 8

Affirmation: *"Doing what you love is the cornerstone of having abundance in your life."* —Wayne Dyer

I love traveling, engaging in intimate conversations, inspiring others and spending time with my husband, family and friends. The more I engage in these activities, the happier and more fulfilled I become.

What do you love doing? How does doing what you love create abundance in your life?

My stepson loves hunting, fishing and being outdoors. He is truly an outdoorsman by all accounts of the word. He becomes his natural, authentic self when he is outside.

Bringing my stepson inside creates a dynamic shift in his behavior. He acts as though he is lost in a foreign country. He doesn't understand or appreciate the rites, rituals and customs of indoor living. Taking off his shoes or cleaning up after himself requires the amount of effort it would take you or me to ask for directions in a Beijing subway. Unfortunately for him, most of his current life's activities are indoors.

It can be challenging, frustrating even exhausting to spend the majority of your existence outside of your preference. The key is to identify the things you love to do then appreciate the moments you have doing what you love.

Personally, we have made adjustments to our family's lifestyle in order to provide my son with more opportunities to be outside. We spend our weekends at the lake, we play family t-ball in the front yard and we go on nightly bike/scooter rides. What adjustments do you need to make to your own life? Do what you **love**. Create **abundance!**

Jill Johns

JUNE 9

Affirmation: *"Truths are the Roots to Trust."*

This affirmation is one that I have used in my home for many years. I felt so strongly about this as a part of our family 'motto' that I painted it on one of the walls in our home. In order for any of us to have healthy, supportive, and compassionate relationships, there must be trust. Trust is a word that far too many take for granted and toss around as if it were a helium balloon left to float away into the great universal unknown. How do we gain and keep trust in our relationships? We can accomplish this by being honest, truthful, loving, kind, compassionate and empathetic.

When we consistently tell the truth to those we love and those in all of our other relationships, we are not only living with integrity but we are building the bonds of trust that will last a lifetime. When it comes to our spouse and/or children, this is especially true. It is akin to taking care of a newly germinated plant. If we feed it what it needs to stay alive, we are helping it to grow strong sturdy roots that will support it in any type of weather. And being honest does not have to hurt. It is not what you say but, more in how you say it. So, all those 'little white lies' you've been telling in order to spare someone's feelings, try another tactic. Anything said in love and kindness is much better received than a lie that can taint even the strongest of relationships.

When we live with truth, we learn to trust and, when we learn to trust, we are not afraid in the world.

Mary M. Romero

JUNE 10

Affirmation: *"Women need real moments of solitude and self reflection to balance out how much of ourselves we give away."* —Barbara De Angelis

It's so great to find your spiritual or quiet place in your house. It really can change your life. Challenge yourself to go in that quiet place once a day, to calm down, to be inspired, and to actually have some peace of mind. It helps you to be more patient, calmer, more grateful, safer, more inspired, and more ways to take care of yourself. Put a fountain in your room, maybe your favorite chair by a big window. Get grounded and open the window and actually listen to the wind, the birds, the trees, and get connected back to nature. You may want to mediate or write in a journal, or even learn how to knit. Get yourself grounded and take some deep breaths. Love yourself and see how that feels. Give yourself the time you deserve. Be your best promoter. When you say "no", that is a complete sentence. Only you really know what you like and what you need. Be your best friend to yourself. You are a child of the most-high God. He has you in the palm of his hands.

Believe!

Angie Schultz

JUNE 11

Affirmation: *Experience is not about what happens to you; it's about what you do with what happens to you.* —Aldous Huxley

Life happens. In your lifetime you will have been disappointed, abandoned, humiliated, betrayed, loved, cherished, and adored. You will have had failures with perhaps bankruptcy, divorce, foreclosure, loss of job, or loss of relationships. You may also have had amazing success with graduating from college (against all odds), starting a business, becoming a wonderful parent, or volunteering.

No matter what the situation, these are all learning experiences. When you fall, dust yourself off, pick yourself up and carry on. With your successes, learn to celebrate and consider what lead to those successes.

Each day of your life provides an opportunity to experience an important lesson.

Linda Ellis Eastman

JUNE 12

Affirmation: *You were given this life because you are strong enough to live it!*

You were given life because you are physically, mentally and spiritually strong enough to live in this space and time. Your life is not an accident as you have been chosen to transcend, change, and awaken your world to the joy of being and make it better simply because you are here.

Cassandra Gaines

JUNE 13

All strange and terrible events are welcome, but comforts we despise.
—Cleopatra

Don't be a Paraskevidekatriaphobic! In other words, don't be afraid of Friday, the 13th! While around 8% or about 20 million people suffer from this phobia, don't allow it to affect what you do or where you go. The Stress Management and Phobia Institute in Asheville, NC estimate that $800 to 900 million dollars in business are lost this day due to the myth of the 13th being an unlucky day. Myths and phobias affect everyone.

The fear of 13 can be traced to different events, combined it created a popular myth and general fear for many. One of the first notations of the number 13 being unlucky comes from a Norse myth when 12 gods were having a dinner party and a 13th uninvited guest showed up. Loki, the uninvited guest, arranged for Hoder, the blind god of darkness to shoot Balder the Beautiful, the god of joy and gladness. Balder died and the earth went dark. The Bible also refers to Judas who betrayed Jesus, as the 13th guest to the Last Supper. In the 12th Century, a religious group was attacked and massacred on Friday the 13th. And, in 1572, there were targeted assassinations on Friday the 13th, which became known as St. Bartholomew's Day massacre. All before the Halloween movies! While these events were after Cleopatra's time, strange and terrible events occurred during and before Cleopatra's reign, 50 to 30 BCE.

Disasters occur, massive rains cause mudslides, floods, tornadoes, hurricanes, large snows, and even strange occurrences like squirrels running across power lines knock out electricity, close down roads, and devastate highways. There is no way to prepare for every situation. Yet, apathy or laziness toward daily needs increases the likelihood of personal problems. Get prepared today. Don't take your safety for granted. Prepare today for disaster.

Katrina Everhart

JUNE 14

Affirmation: *Ignite new energy!* —Kimberly May

My friend and colleague, Kimberly May, shared this with me recently. I was so inspired by it and thought it might be meaningful for you!

"This morning I lit several white candles on my mantle for family members, my business, and a new white candle for new possibilities. As I was trying to light the last candle, I had to drop the match because it was so hot and about to go out, it fell right next to the wick but it didn't light the candle. I watched the match burn on both ends wishing it would light the wick but it didn't, though it was so close. I continued to pray for a moment. Then as it was just about to go out, I thought maybe there was something else I could do. I picked up the candle and tilted it just a little. Just as the match was about to go out, it lit the wick and the most beautiful flame took hold! I cried. I can see how in my own life, I get so close to a goal, dream or idea, feeling like I am burning it from both ends, and so ready to give up and yet so close to reaching my goal!

This was such a perfect lesson for me today. I wanted to share it with you just in case you are so close or feeling like you want to give up. Please don't! You are right where you are suppose to be. It might just take a moment of prayer or gratitude, leaning in a little closer, letting go, or just taking one more step in the right direction to ignite new energy for yourself and your life and finally reaching that goal, moving you in a whole new direction!"

Kim Evans

JUNE 15

Affirmation: *The pessimist complains about the wind; the optimist expects it to change and the realist adjusts the sails.* —William Arthur Ward

No matter what life presents to you, be prepared to change your course if you must. Never be stuck in a rut or handling situations a certain way. Rather than facing challenges with a negative point of view, know there is always an answer and steer into a new course of action that will take you where you want to go.

Linda Ellis Eastman

JUNE 16

"Our deepest wishes are whispers of our authentic selves. We must learn to respect them. We must learn to listen." —Sarah Ban Breathnach

When you believe in yourself, so do others.

You have a positive view of life that others find attractive. You must believe in your ability to be successful in any situation. When others see this high level of confidence, they believe in your ability to be successful, too.

You should only allow positive thoughts to enter into your mind. You should regularly imagine yourself being successful and fully expect success in everything you do. Each success breeds future successes.

From time to time, you may find yourself struggling, just like everyone else. But you should always maintain belief in yourself. Your self-confidence should be unshaken in any and all circumstances. It should feel natural to believe in yourself.

Believe in your ability to conquer any challenge that occurs in your life. You are a survivor. You will thrive in challenging situations. Others can sense the level of belief you have in yourself, and it makes them believe in you even more.

Affirmation: *Today, I release any self-doubt I may harbor.* ***I believe in my abilities and in my potential for success.*** *I can see how much others believe in me, as well, when I believe in myself.*

Judith Duclot-Fletcher

JUNE 17

Act Enthusiastic and You'll BE Enthusiastic!

How many times do we say something like, "I'll do _____, once I get the energy for it." We tend to believe that something has to happen TO us or FOR us in order to draw up our energy or enthusiasm. Indeed, the opposite is true.

At one point during my busy career, the only feasible time for me to get a workout in was at 5:30 am. Even for most morning people like me, this is still early! It was easy to make excuses why I couldn't go to the gym, or believe I would just find time later in the day. That make-up workout rarely ever happened. So, this became a mental game. I knew I had to work out early in the morning or it wouldn't get done. Skipping my workout was not acceptable to me either. So when the alarm sounded at 5:30, I had to make my body move despite my mind telling me to stay in bed. Without fail, during each early workout, I developed the energy for it only AFTER I spent 10 minutes getting going. Not before. I needed to get moving in order to find the energy to keep going. When I waited to find the energy to start, it never came.

And so it is with any task. By merely starting the activity, before long the energy for it develops. What are you waiting on that you really should have started already? What have you been procrastinating on that would really make a difference in your life? You will find boundless enthusiasm, just by getting started!

Rebecca Sheperd

JUNE 18

"Freedom is never voluntarily given by the oppressor; it must be demanded by the oppressed." —Martin Luther King Jr.

Today is Juneteenth, better known as Emancipation Day for black Americans. It commemorates the announcement of the abolition of slavery in the state of Texas, but is celebrated broadly as a day of freedom for blacks across the country. The name Juneteenth is derived from the words "June" and "nineteenth" and is recognized as a special day of observance.

Although the Emancipation Proclamation was issued by President Abraham Lincoln in 1862 with an effective date of January 1, 1863, it wasn't until June 18, 1865—as the American Civil War wound down—that federal troops arrived in Galveston, Texas, to enforce the law and free the slaves. Can you imagine? Word (and legal force) took two years to be put into effect!

Juneteenth compels me to say: You are *free*! You have the freedom to live the life of which you've uniquely dreamed; you are free to live without judgment and directives from oppressors. You are free to be in control of your own outcomes. You have the right to live free of danger and persecution. You are free to define your life's boundaries and live in them fully.

Thank God for the freedoms that we take for granted in this day and time in history. Many before us weren't granted such liberties. Today, you have the right to question the things that oppress or hold you back in your life. You have the right to fight for the life that you want. What a wonderful blessing!

Dawn Jamison

JUNE 19

"A woman is the full circle. Within her is the power to create, nurture and transform." —Diane Mariechild

You are your own unique self - special, creative, and wonderful.

You are unique in the universe. Your Creator made you with a special intention in mind. You are special, creative, and wonderful. Remembering these ideas will help you strive to reach your full potential.

Of all the people in the world, you are the only one that is exactly like you. Your unique qualities and talents are gifts, and it is up to you to develop them to share with others and better the world around you.

It can be challenging to be different from others. But you will appreciate and embrace your uniqueness. *Your value to the world is directly related to your ability to demonstrate that you are one of a kind.*

Each day, you should become more confident that you are special. *You have the strength to let the world see your true self.* Be proud of who you are.

Affirmation: *Today, I am willing to embrace my uniqueness and that of others as well. Each one of us, including me, is special, creative, and wonderful. It is up to me to show everyone how special I am.*

Judith Duclot-Fletcher

JUNE 20

Affirmation: *"When the grass appears greener on the other side of the fence, fertilize your grass."* —Edge Keynote

Have you ever longingly desired to posses some of the talents and gifts of a friend, relative or colleague? Or have you desired to look great like your friend who works out at the gym? Perhaps you may have wished for a new car, home or vacation? Sometimes we want what we don›t have; wishing, comparing or competing will not solve the dilemma.

When you water, fertilize and nurture your lawn, it will be healthy. Without proper care, your lawn will not survive. As an individual, your mind, body and emotions also need proper care; take time to feed and nurture you.

This is the time to assess and take inventory of your own life! What gives you pleasure, joy and satisfaction? As women, we are often in the caretaker role taking care of others first and then ourselves.

When you fertilize our own grass, you will experience a healthier mind and body and ultimately healthier relationships.

Lori Tsugawa Whaley

JUNE 21

Look for God's gifts.

This was Father's Day in 2009. We had finished breakfast and opened daddy's gifts, and it was time for me to hit the shower. No sooner did I wet my hair, when my 4 and 6 year old daughters ran in to tell me Daddy had fallen and he was seriously hurt. I dried off, ran downstairs to find him completely passed out on the floor, not breathing, lifeless. The paramedics tried to revive him, but to no avail. Daddy died that day from a pulmonary embolism: a blood clot resulting from a recent knee surgery. I became a widow and single mother at once in that moment. My children lost their father in that moment. The world lost a very good man in that moment. We would never be the same.

God gave me several gifts that day. I first discovered a deep and resounding inner strength that I didn't know existed within me. It helped me guide my daughters and myself during our grieving. God also reminded me how much He loves me. I felt His love so completely and fully during my deepest and darkest moments to follow. This gave me peace, which passes all understanding. Another gift. Finally, I was given a realization on that day: that my life has meaning and purpose, and that God has significant plans for me to make an impact in this world.

Someone told me that God took my husband because he had fulfilled God's plan for him on this earth, and he was now needed in Heaven. That resounded with me. It confirmed my sense that I am not yet finished doing God's work here on earth, so I had better get moving! What is your significant purpose in this world? Have you gotten started yet? People are in need of your gifts and talents. Go make your difference in this world! Start today.

Rebecca Sheperd

JUNE 22

Affirmation: *"Between two evils, I always pick the one I never tried before."*
—Mae West

Mae West, early screen goddess with an attitude. She was known to be outspoken when women weren't and opinionated when that was not acceptable in women.

Sometimes life hands you a lemon, and there is no tequila and salt handy. You are faced with a choice. Neither of them appeals. Do what Mae West recommends, and make the choice that you wouldn't normally make. Take the action you would never do. You don't know where that path leads, because you have never trod it before.

Sometimes, the only thing to do, is to do something differently. Take a different path. Try a different attitude, thought pattern, or belief. It might open up an entirely new option for you, when you thought you had none at all.

Take a different path. At the very least, you will see something you have never seen before, even if there is no escaping the outcome.

Becky Paroz

JUNE 23

Affirmation: *"Just because someone else has an issue does not mean that you have to make it an 'issue' for yourself. Only own what is yours, no one else's."*

We, as women, seem to have this innate desire to want to please everyone all the time! Unfortunately, or, fortunately, depending on how you want to look at it, this is not possible. We know this so why, why, why, do we continue to beat ourselves up because of someone else's feelings? Well, today is the day you decide to make life that much more enjoyable, free, and liberating than before by simply owning what is yours and no one else's!

Your teenager misses an important school assignment. You do not need to try to pick up the pieces, write the teacher a note, run to the store to get supplies, etc. Your child missed the assignment, you did not! Let them own it and learn from it. Your in-laws decided not to come to a family reunion and are now receiving 'heat' from other family members. Your in-laws made the decision, you did not! You do not need to stay on the phone for hours with various family members making excuses for them. They made the choice, point the 'questioners' in their direction and let them own their own decision. You decided you were too tired this week to do your routine work-out that you know makes you feel better and less stressed. Now, you are stressing over missing that workout and beating yourself up for it. *You* made that decision, no one else, own it! So you missed a week, what is that compared to a lifetime? Don't take your anger at yourself out on others. Own your decision, make sure you continue to make time for yourself and your outlet and then *let it go*!

Free yourself from the burdens that others would like to share with you. Sharing is good but, not when it comes to our mental and emotional health. Owning our own is hard enough. Let go of something you have been taking on as your own today, see how much lighter your day feels!

Mary M. Romero

176

JUNE 24

Affirmation: *"'Thank you' is the best prayer that anyone could say.
I say that one a lot. Thank you expresses extreme gratitude,
humility, understanding."* —Alice Walker

I remember the first time I read The Secret by Rhonda Byrne, I was shocked and amazed by the simplicity of the message. The concept that impressed me the most is a very simple concept and it has become a part of my daily routine. Each morning, as I step out of bed, as I place my right foot down I say "thank." As I place my left foot I say "you." As I approach the bathroom, and consequently the rest of my day, I repeat (right) thank, (left) you, (right) thank, (left) you, thank, you, thank, you, thank, you.

Starting with gratitude sets the stage for the rest of your day. It opens your heart. It reminds you that although you may have slept poorly, have a tight back, have bad knees or have a busy day ahead, you should be grateful for your abundance. Saying thank you reminds you that life is a gift in and of itself. Thank you is the simplest form of prayer. Thank you is the simplest form of appreciation. Thank you is the simplest form of acknowledging and accepting the life you have been given.

I make it a regular practice to send hand-written thank you notes. I don't just send them for the material gifts I receive, but for the help, the gestures and the kindnesses that I receive as well. Sending hand-written thank you notes to colleagues, employees, friends, family and even your children will leave a long-lasting favorable impression and will make life a little bit sweeter for everyone.

Who should you thank today?

Jill Johns

JUNE 25

For all the little girls out there following their dreams…the artists, the musicians, the passionate entrepreneurs, the authors, the doctors, the teachers… and especially my beautiful daughters, Katy and Lindsay.

I see a girl.
12 years old.
She asks her parents if she can try out for the basketball team.
They say yes.

She gets her own basketball and a special pair of shoes.
And she practices. And practices. And practices.
Her dad pours a concrete slab in front of his garage and puts up a hoop.
And she practices. And practices. And practices.

And she goes to camps.
And she practices. And practices. And practices.
Teams. Awards. Accolades for skill.
Love of the game.

And practice.

Her secret to success.

Dr. Joanne Siebert, D.C.

JUNE 26

Affirmation: *"I create space for people to be who they are."*

Everyone wants to be accepted as they are, without judgment or criticism. That goes for you, too. By creating space for people to be themselves, you provide an opportunity for full self-expression by each person. You welcome and invite the unique qualities that make them who they are. When you judge and criticize others, it is more about you than them. It highlights aspects of yourself that you have not accepted and illuminates the areas that require time and attention to fully embrace. It takes different people with different characteristics, strengths, talents and gifts to make the world go around.

Refrain from judgment and criticism. Celebrate what is unique about you and the people in your life and be open to the richness that full self-expression provides.

Michelle Richardson

JUNE 27

Affirmation: *"Who says, Diamonds are only a girl's best friend? Shine 'bright like a diamond', show your many facets and the universe will fall in love with you!"*

Dedicated to my sister, Gigi. You are a gem, shine bright!

Take one moment today to think of your world. Then, take a moment to think of the entire world and its many different cultures, sub-cultures, races, ethnicities, backgrounds, and diversities. In order for our universe to work in sync, we must all contribute whatever our gift is. YOU are amazingly unique and there is only one of you in the entire world! YOU possess gifts and talents that no one else does. Like the many facets to a gem that started out as a rock, you have shined your gifts, talents, and experiences that make up who you are. The world deserves to see your beauty! And you deserve to be a shining example in everyone's life that you come across. For, without you, this universe could not function and be in sync.

I have a set of identical twins yet, it is not the make-up, clothes they wear, or even the fact that they look identical that makes them special. It is the unique gifts that each one possesses; their personalities, likes, dislikes, interests, loving and giving hearts, laughter and kindness.... these are the shining facets that the world see's and what sets them apart even from themselves. You are a rare beauty that is uniquely, perfectly, you. Shine bright, my friend!

Mary M. Romero

JUNE 28

I choose to celebrate my life!

I read somewhere that what I focus on expands. The biblical version is 'you reap what you sow'. A dear friend of mine once told me, "You see it, you be it!"

If that's the case, it is important that I choose to **celebrate** my life, every nuance, every crazy-making moment, every upside down path… seeing all of the chapters in my story as a celebration of life, full out!

And, if I focus on 'celebration', then that is what expands.

That celebration is what I reap.

I see it, I be it!

Celebrate with me right now…for wherever two or more gathered!

Repeat after me:

I see it.

I be it.

I see it.

I be it.

I see it.

I be it.

I can do this. You can do this.

Sharon McWilliams

JUNE 29

Affirmation: *"If you obey all the rules you miss all the fun"*.
—Katharine Hepburn

Life is filled with rules, especially as a woman. We are raised to be "nice", to look and smell good, to be feminine, to be strong, etc etc. I am sure you can think of a few rules that you were taught, or continue to be held to.

Have you ever stopped and questioned the rules? Katherine Hepburn did. She refused to be a "good girl", she wore men's pants in time when that was shocking to society. She smoked, she drank, and she gave her love to whom she chose, not necessarily according to the rules of society. I am pretty sure she had a lot of fun in her life.

What are you missing out on because you obey "the rules"? Who made these rules? I have never read the rule book myself, so I make up my own rules. Some of them are around not hurting people, which I think is a good rule. Some of them are around what I am supposed to be in my work life, and I break those all the time.

I once had a friend ask me, "why can't I just be a good girl"? Because I don't buy into that rule. It doesn't work for me. That's just no fun.

Check the rules that you are living by that perhaps don't serve you any more – and then break them! Enjoy it thoroughly.

Becky Paroz

JUNE 30

"The key to change is to let go of fear." —Rosanne Cash

Any form of change can prompt fear to take over and paralyze you but you must stop fear in its tracks so that you can fulfill your purpose and move toward your desired goals. It is important to know the difference between fear and fact. Fear is *false evidence appearing real.* **For every fear, there is a fact;** a *full and complete truth.*

When you are faced with fear; there is a present truth, if you will embrace it. Whether you are starting a new project, new job, going to college or any other life change; fear will whisper inadequacy but fact says that you can do it! While you may have some challenges or setbacks that threaten to hinder your plans or progress; don't give up. Choose instead to face the fear and forge ahead.

Your reward or goal will outweigh the fear but you will not know it until you try. Adopting a 'can-do' attitude will help you overcome your fears and catapult you into a positive direction.

Be inspired to let go of all self-limiting thoughts, face your fears and move forward.

Affirmation: *I will let go of my fears.*

Frenetta Tate

JULY 1

Affirmation: *"I am fully present with whomever and whatever is in front of me."*

There are few gifts greater than the gift of giving someone or something your full attention. Life can be full of distractions if you allow it to be. The temptation to fill your life up to the point of distraction is a real and often appealing one. The prices for such a choice are significant; stress, low quality relationships and reduced productivity, to name a few. Commit to being fully present your norm. Notice when you become distracted and bring yourself back to whomever or whatever you were engaged in at the time.

Make being connected and fully present a priority. Meditate, focus on one thing at a time, engage actively in conversations, and give each one your undivided attention. In doing so, you and the people in your life will reap significant benefits.

Michelle Richardson

JULY 2

Affirmation: *"Have you ever had a moment of clarity in the middle of an emotional storm? Hold onto that tool that helped you get there....you'll need it for the future!"*

Have you ever been in the middle of a crisis situation and, BAM! Out of nowhere came a moment of clarity? These times don't happen too often for me but, it is akin to seeing the sun shine through a rainstorm.... you receive an answer you were seeking, without even realizing it. Your spirit was open and calling for help. You can thank whatever you believe in whether that be a higher power, God, the universe or, your own gut instinct. We are all made of such enormously intense energy that, sometimes, in our deepest, darkest hour, we are lifted up by an invisible force. If we all realize that what we put out into the world, we will receive back, how much more would we all feel connected?

Don't lose that connection that seems to only come in a time of crisis. Keep your spirit open to the energies, love, and all that can be good in this world…you never know when you will need the support.

Mary M. Romero

JULY 3

Affirmation: *"I encourage open, honest communication by leading the way."*

Communication is among the most important, yet scarcely developed skills many people possess. People can go through their entire lives devoid of critical communication skills that contribute to self-confidence, self-esteem, self-expression, and high quality relationships. Many people hesitate to have open, honest conversations for fear of offending, conflict, or losing something. Ironically, it is by effectively communicating that we, our relationships, and our careers thrive. It takes a strong, confident person to take this approach; be that person. Lead by example through open honest communication and prepare for deeper, more meaningful relationships and levels of success.

Choose a situation in which open, honest communication would serve you well (even if it scares you). Review the information at http://bit.ly/mwiCommunicate and complete the exercise before having the conversation.

Michelle Richardson

JULY 4

Practice positive thinking.

When I worked for a leadership development company, I was responsible for sales and client development. This required me to learn how to accept rejection. Not an easy thing to master (indeed, I am still working on that)! A particular sales call had me rattled and I went to my mentor for help. She advised, "Don't let that person or experience live rent-free in your head! Raise the rent and kick him out!" What sage advice. How could I project confidence and empowerment for the next call if negative thoughts and experiences from this one were crowding the space in my head? Rent-free, no less! I needed to evict the negative emotion coming from that one negative sales call in order to refresh and renew my confidence to keep going.

So, I started looking at the accomplishments I had already made. This helped me see that I was very capable to make sales happen. I contacted a supportive client and engaged in a productive conversation surrounding their business, which reminded me that I was good at building relationships, even if one call didn't go so well. And I read books on positive thinking and empowerment to build my confidence up again, to invade my mind with positive thoughts so there wouldn't be any space for the negative ones. It worked. Eviction notice: signed, sealed and delivered!

Rebecca Sheperd

JULY 5

"When we speak we are afraid our words will not be heard or welcomed. But when we are silent, we are still afraid. So it is better to speak."
—Audre Lorde

You can find the bright side in a crisis.

You are leaving behind your instinct to succumb to situations that fall apart around you. *The moments that attempt to foil your optimism now bring you into the hopeful sky of opportunity instead.*

You owe myself the effort to look beyond the obvious circumstances. Look for the goodness and positivity that are also present, shining brightly beyond the shadows.

The more effort you exert to find the silver lining in your despair, the easier it is for you to stay positive in any situation.

When you feel like giving in, remind yourself to seek that silver lining. Focusing on your search helps to keep you from dwelling on the negative. By standing up for your desire for optimism, you change your aura and enlighten those around you.

Affirmation: *Today, I face my challenges with positivity. I am fortunate to have come to this insight about choosing optimism. In the end, my mind, body, and soul reap the benefits of my positive thinking.*

Judith Duclot-Fletcher

JULY 6

Affirmation: *"A man who views the world the same at fifty as he did at twenty has wasted thirty years of his life"*. —Muhammad Ali

Muhammad Ali is one of the most famous boxers of all time. He was an African American and a Muslim at a time when it was not acceptable to be either of those things in the world. He overcame the many difficulties that were raised to be one of the most famous sportsmen in his field.

He knew that if he had stayed the same person, kept to the same lessons that he was taught as a boy, he never would have taken that leap of faith it took to become the heroic inspiration that he remains today.

Do you have beliefs that no longer serve you? Do you follow the teachings of your childhood, your schooling, your environment because you choose to, or because you think you should, or because it never occurred to you to question those teachings?

As life changes, knowledge increases. When you gain knowledge, you are not the same person any more, you have been expanded, increased. Be open to it. Be open to the changes that may follow. It may be the very thing to get you to that next goal, the next level in your career, the life you dream for yourself.

Don't think you know everything and that you can only do something one way. Go for the outcome you want, but allow the manner in which you achieve to be flexible so as to learn along the journey itself. Be open to change. Don't waste your life clinging to beliefs, thoughts and actions that no longer serve who you are.

Make a plan to look at life differently each and every day, you might be surprised and pleased by what you see.

Becky Paroz

JULY 7

Affirmation: *"Remember that you are unique. If that is not fulfilled, then something wonderful has been lost."* —Martha Graham

You are a unique and marvelous individual and there is no one in the world that is exactly like you! With your individual talents and gifts, there is a purpose that only you can fulfill.

In the movie, "It's a Wonderful Life," a man discovers what life would be like without him and realizes his impact. His friends and family would have a different life and it would not be complete. Whether you think of yourself as a piece of a puzzle, an instrument in an orchestra or yarn in a beautiful tapestry, you are vitally important. Imagine your life without some of your loved ones; it would not be the same and each person holds a special place in your life.

During your life's journey, you will continue to discover, develop, 'fine-tune' and unwrap your individual present(s) for the good of mankind. Acknowledge your significant gift(s) and you as an individual, just like you acknowledge your loved ones and friends!

Lori Tsugawa Whaley

JULY 8

Affirmation: *"Happiness is an attitude. We either make ourselves miserable, or happy and strong. The amount of work is the same."*
—Francesca Reigler

Today, I want to share with you a fun way to illustrate the value of a positive attitude.

We know that hard work and knowledge are vital to success. Yet, you have likely heard that attitude makes all the difference. Just how important is attitude? What allows us to give 100%? This mathematical formula shows us.

If:

A B C D E F G H I J K L M N O P Q R S T U V W X Y Z

Is represented as:

1 2 3 4 5 6 7 8 9 10 11 12 13 14 15 16 17 18 19 20 21 22 23 24 25 26

Then:

H-A-R-D-W-O-R-K = 8+1+18+4+23+15+18+11=98%

and

K-N-O-W-L-E-D-G-E = 11+14+15+23+12+5+4+7+5=96%

However

A-T-T-I-T-U-D-E = 1+20+20+9+20+21+4+5=100%

Therefore, the math shows that hardwork and knowledge are valuable and will get you close to 100%, however, attitude is the thing that makes the difference and gets you there!

Janet Christensen

JULY 9

Affirmation: *"Humor is one of the best ingredients of survival".*
                                                —Aung San Suu Kyi

Aung San Suu Kyi spent 15 years in custody in Burma, her native land, for her outspokenness against the brutal rule of her country. She had the option to leave her country if she would but promise to keep her mouth shut about the dictatorship in her country (and never return). She refused. She remained in her country, in trouble and under house arrest for most of the time.

In 2012, after all her years of fighting, arrests, convictions and threats against her life, she finally won the freedom for her country she had been working for and took office.

During this time, she was awarded a Nobel Peace Prize, and Congressional Medal of Honour and the International Simón Bolívar Prize, amongst many.

One can only imagine what life must have been life for her, watching the horrors inflicted upon her fellow country men and women, not to mention her personal circumstance.

If anyone is qualified to tell us how to survive, it is this amazing woman. And I agree with her. When all else fails, just laugh. When it gets too much, give over to humour. Laughter and humour release 'feel-good' chemicals in our body, which can help when those black moods strike. The ability to laugh in the face of our troubles gives us the ability to look at our problems another way. It gives you back your power, when it seems like you have none.

Laugh, survive, breathe. Then live and laugh again.

Becky Paroz

JULY 10

Affirmation: *"Peace begins with a smile."* —Mother Teresa

We are often so busy and frantic that we often have scowls on our faces from the stress and pressure of our schedule.

We fill our schedules with all of our "to-dos" but we often fail to schedule in time to simply stop and enjoy the moment. Our reactions to our world around us and what we feel we must accomplish causes us stress and turmoil. We often make excuses as to why we cannot slow down.

But running on the treadmill of life does not bring us happiness or contentment; it is acknowledging the perfection of the moment. Slow down and bring your attention back to this moment and recognize the beauty of the quietness.

Start your day to day with a conscious smile on your face and recognize you are taking the first step toward your inner peace today.

Maritza Rodriguez-Arseneau

JULY 11

Great minds discuss ideas; average minds discuss events;
small minds discuss people. —Eleanor Roosevelt

Gossip abounds in today's workplace and at community events. And, in many cases gossip in the workplace and in communities is no less than bullying in school. Folks use gossip as a way to maintain behavior by exerting force on individuals to be average or maintain the status quo. Yet, the status quo is often how folks lose money, lose the respect of others, and find themselves in trouble.

And, while we like averages in some cases because we are above them; we dislike averages when we are considered below average in other things. Average helps us know what is mainstream. They help us determine safety issues, such as 120 over 80 is average, but considered normal for blood pressure. Yet individuals vary. Above the norm is bad; Below can be bad as well. Above average weight is bad, below is bad as well. Both, means the more likely the person is to have health problems.

Interestingly these days, we shoot for average. Folks feel alright with average. We discuss people and events at work, at night, and on the weekends because it is easier to do. Yet, easy does not help us get promotions. It does not help us get business funding to start a business. Talking about others can get us into trouble if the information can be proven untrue and the person takes us to court.

Commit yourself today to discussing ideas to help yourself and your community.

Katrina Everhart

JULY 12

Affirmation: *"Women need real moments of solitude and self-reflection to balance out how much of ourselves we give away."* —Barbara de Angelis

Alone time. What a novel idea! What I wouldn't do to get a few moments of solitude for self-reflection. Ideally, I would sit in lotus, burn some candles, shut my eyes, listen to my breathing and reflect about the abundance I have in my life. Like I said, that would be ideal.

In reality, I get my moments of solitude on my commute to and from work each day. I have spent the last 7+ years driving over 60 minutes one way to get to work. While driving may not be the ideal situation for self-reflection, I have learned to use that time effectively and to cherish it. Many of life's problems have been solved on the way to and from work each day.

When can you find moments of solitude for self-reflection in your life? Here are a few suggestions:
- The first 5 waking minutes of the day.
- While waiting in line at your favorite coffee shop.
- Standing in line at the grocery store.
- Waiting to pick your children up at the end of the school day.
- The last 10 minutes before you fall asleep.

What can you do during that time?
- Take a moment to say thank you for the abundance you have been given.
- Acknowledge and validate yourself for all of your hard work.
- Count your blessings.
- Set goals for yourself for that day or the next day.

The small moments of solitude can add up over the course of the day. Go ahead and give yourself that gift. You deserve it!

Jill Johns

JULY 13

If you want to see what your body will look like tomorrow, examine your thoughts today. —Navajo Proverb

We have a thousand thoughts per minute – some to do items, some dreams, some hopes, some positive, many negative. Your thoughts today determine your tomorrow. Your thoughts not only manage and control your actions, they affect your body! Notice how some folks look younger and act younger than their biological age? Notice how some folks seem old in their 20s because of what they say and do?

Just yesterday someone told me they were having trouble. They noted I just did not understand because I was too young. Turned out, I was 13 years older than they were! They decided that if I looked this good ...they had made themselves old. Interestingly, they felt we had the same situations, but made different choices. They said they always used a simple pros and cons method. Yet this method is too simple to make life choices. By using the wrong decision making method, this person had chosen the life they had. Using a more robust and appropriate decision making method such as a Decision tree, or a Grid Analysis, they felt they would have been in a better situation. Sometimes the simplest choices should not be made quickly. Think about fast food, its quick, easy, and cheap, but folks often gain lots of weight.

Negative thoughts can be re-organized. Research has noted that smiling for just a few seconds releases endorphins that change blood pressure and mood for over two hours. Folks who watch funny movies or funny shows heal faster than those who do not. The body cannot tell whether laughter is fake or real. Laughter even for 30 seconds helps the brain and changes your mood. Laughter Yoga, combines exercise and laughter. Twitters, guffaws, smerks, and belly laughs change with the exercises. Programmed or not, find a way to laugh.

Katrina Everhart

JULY 14

"Be kind, for everyone you meet is fighting a harder battle." —Plato

"The only way out of the labyrinth of suffering is to forgive."
—John Green, Looking for Alaska

As I aged; I saw first-hand how much energy that being negative took out of you each day. I saw families turn on each other. Siblings that refused to be compassionate in their dealings with each other or worse would not forgive OLD hurts.

My sister Mitzie was my example with this trait. She was older and I being younger was VERY annoying to her just by being me. When I went off to college, she called our Mother to ask if I was keeping in touch and was I okay since I went to college. She had just read an article that said the quiet people you know were usually the ones that struggled with suicide the most and no one ever knew it. She immediately thought of me as I was the quietest person she knew! Well of course our Mother immediately got off the phone and called me.

After I asked Momma why she was calling, she fessed up and I laughed so hard. She was immediately upset wanted to know how I was; who I talked to if I was upset, etc. I finally got her to admit that Mitzi was the one that was really worried. And I felt compassion and forgiveness from Mitzie even though she wasn't the one that called.

Even today, she oozes compassion and forgiveness in all that she does and says. I look to her as my daily example of what I want to be like in the future!

Michele McLeskey

JULY 15

"Don't dwell on those who let you down, cherish those who hold you up."
—Author Unknown

Life is too short for us to squander away precious moments in an environment where we find ourselves compromising who we are to fit in, be liked, accepted or validated. Instead of "fitting in" to please others, I choose to be true to me so… I "go where I am celebrated not tolerated." Choosing that path makes my life journey more pleasurable and less complicated.

Shirley A Williams

JULY 16

Affirmation: *"Build the trust in your relationships....it starts with 'being there'....always!"*

We are all aware that relationships take work if we want them to be successful, supportive and long lasting. But do we really know what "being there" really means? I will share a very brief story on how to ruin a perfectly good relationship! I was visiting my sister, many years ago, in California. She wanted to introduce me to a friend of hers she had recently met so, we went to her home and sat outside chatting a while. A while turned into the longest three hours of my life (up to that point). When we left, I realized that I had sat and talked to this woman for three hours but she didn't say a WORD! I don't mean that she didn't speak....she spoke but, it was like a bunch of garbled words thrown together to mean absolutely nothing. I remember saying to myself, "Oh my gosh....I just talked to someone for 3 hours and she said absolutely nothing! How does that happen??" It happens when we are 'there' in body but not in mind or spirit.

How many times have you had a conversation with someone and they simply did not hear a word you said proved by the lack of response and/or emotion? In order for all of our relationships to be mutually healthy, we must be sure to 'be there' not only in body but, in mind and spirit. We must be fully engaged while listening as well as talking. If we are not, we leave the receiver in the relationship feeling unheard, uncared for, and hurt. This goes for all relationships from a spouse, daughter, mother, father, son, co-worker, as well as the person behind the register! This is one of the ways we show we are trustworthy and worth that person spending their time on us. Everyone's time is precious. Have respect for each individual as they are and be engaged. You will notice just how far a simple nod of the head can go when someone simply feels heard.

Mary M. Romero

JULY 17

Affirmation: *I will value my relationships.*

How long have you ben married? How old were you when you got married? Sometimes we pick someone we marry who is the hard parent or wasn't there for us, or controlling, or unfair. We pick a partner just like our mom or our dad. Why? Because it's so familiar, so easy, so comfortable. Have you ever done that? You may not even know you did that until you are married, twenty, thirty, or forty years. One day you wake up and said, "Who is my husband? I don't even know who he is!" Why? Because you woke up, got a bigger life and changed. That changed everything. Thank goodness you woke up. You can stop and recognize the abuse now. You didn't even know it was happening. There are no mistakes; you have to be awake to get it though. Go get a bigger life for you. Find your passion and go do what you love. It's never too late to make a change and just get a bigger life. I'm not saying leave your husband, but change the pattern. Do what you want now. Go to a movie by yourself or go to dinner. Feel what its like to do what you want for you. By you finding your bigger life and making you happy it may cause your relationship with your husband to be more fun and more interesting, because you are taking care of yourself. He had a life, working, doing what he loves so maybe its time to do what you want. It's now or never. If you don't go try you will ever know. Don't have regrets. Be fearless. Jump in the fire and do it anyway. Live today!

Angie Schultz

JULY 18

Treat your family like friends and your friends like family.
—Proverb Quote.

"There are the families that we are born into, and there are the families that we choose; our circle of friends. While their faces may change over the course of our lives, the joy they bring us remains constant." —Anonymous

Friends are like the Wild flowers of our personal gardens. They grow where they are called by God to grow. God is infinitely more intelligent, intuitive and way kinder than I, so I'll defer to him in their location and number.

If you are a gardener, you KNOW how much work a garden can be. As a Gardener you have to use TLC from start to finish. Love goes in to selecting the site, preparing the area for planting, planting then watching & defending against weeds and other pests all the way through to lovingly harvesting the fruit and vegetables as they are ready. Each step of the process requires great attention to detail for any abnormalities or threats.

I have not always tended my garden of friends so I am left with reaping what I have sown in the past. Having a GOOD friend is like having a sister, but having a GREAT friend is like having a twin sister who can read your mind and never condemns you choices. I have a few friends through my own ignorance, negligence and general thoughtlessness. For these friends, I pray for forgiveness from God and the chance to do better in the future with new friends he will bring me!

Friends are a blessing in and among themselves but when that friend is your sister you are blessed infinitely. My little sister, Kathy DeeAnn McLeskey Cheney, is the most wonderful example of solid friendship I could ever have.

Michele McLeskey

JULY 19

"The question isn't who's going to let me; it's who is going to stop me."
—Ayn Rand

Living life to the fullest will bring you happiness.

You should love your life. ***Each day brings its own special set of treasures, adventures, and interesting encounters.*** Pay attention to the gems that come your way, such as compliments, smiles from strangers, and unexpected occurrences.

When you get a chance to try something new, take the plunge and do it. You will love the idea that you can make every effort to engage in something that's shiny and new to you.

You must believe that every new experience will expands your mind. Make it a point to pay attention, make eye contact, and have a pleasing look on your face when you are around others. Living life to the fullest means you are "on" and connected to others at every opportunity. The more you engage with others, the happier you will feel.

Affirmation: *Today, my plan is to have my arms and mind wide open to all that life delivers. I want to grab onto everything that comes my way and live my life to the fullest. As I embrace my life and all that it entails, I feel happier and happier.*

Judith Duclot-Fletcher

JULY 20

Affirmation: *"Some of the most successful leaders are also the best listeners."*
—Mary Kay Ash

In Dallas, Texas, 50 years ago, Mary Kay Ash started with her life savings, a few products in a tiny store and one big dream. She began writing a book to help women in the corporate world; it became the business plan for her successful company, Mary Kay Cosmetics.

One of Mary Kay›s principles is to listen and discover what women want to serve them better. Listening is a learned skill. Listening is a necessary skill to become an effective leader. Mary Kay believed in empowering women and Mary Kay is an American success story! In 2013, the company celebrated 50 fabulous years and still going strong with many women driving pink Cadillacs living their dream!

Have you wondered why you have two ears and one mouth? When you listen to your clients, colleagues and loved ones, you validate them and will experience a mutually beneficial conversation while building rapport.

If you desire to be an effective and successful leader, become a good listener.

Lori Tsugawa Whaley

JULY 21

Affirmation: *While death may take away the physical presence, your loved one remains strong in your heart, mind, and consciousness.* (adapted from Rev. Anne Marie Evers, Vancouver, Canada)

My mother passed away on this day, some five years ago following a long battle with parkinson's disease. While she suffered deeply, she never complained and held hard onto her personal independence with as much humour as she could muster. Yet, while I cannot talk to her, I can hear her voice and I can still listen to her advice. I can visualize her busily canning fruits and vegetables, all products of her well tended garden. I can visualize her preparing a Thanksgiving or Christmas dinner and I can see her busy knitting her special little caps that captured so many women's desires.

I keep one of my mother's special china tea cups in my family room so that she has a presence in my heart and mind every day. She is with me when I confront a challenge. I can ask myself, "how would mother handle this?" and the answer will come to me. It's comforting to know she is still there for me.

However, I know some women did not have good relationships with their mother. I ask that you find a way to forgive and forget any past wrongdoings. Some mothers may not have been perfect because their own life's teachings didn't give them the lessons they needed to learn. Learn from these lessons and make different choices in your life. Remember, that while death may take away the physical presence, your mother will remain strong in your heart, mind, and consciousness

Barbara J. Bowes, FCHRP. CMC, CCP, M.Ed

JULY 22

Affirmation: *"Food is to the Body What Love is to the Soul.
Feed Your Soul!"*

We all know in order to live long, happy, healthy lives, it begins with the nutrition we put into our bodies and the exercise to keep us fit. Sure, who doesn't like a big, moist piece of chocolate cake or a freshly glazed donut right off the conveyor belt or even a nice big bowl of ice-cream and a good movie?! As my grandfather of 102 years-old always told me, "Mary, everything in moderation….just don't overdo it!"

We can find all types of information on healthy lifestyles, what is good for us and what is not, what can help with this ailment or that health issue but, what of our spirit and soul? Our souls and our spirits need 'nutritional love' just as our bodies have needs. While you are busy keeping yourself healthy and fit in body, remember to never neglect that which every living being needs to survive; love, compassion, and caring. Never be afraid to feed your soul that which it longs for and deserves. It not only feels good to receive love but, is an amazing feeling when we can share that love and caring with another. So, when you get that hunger or a taste for something, you're just not sure what it is….listen to your spirit and feed your soul, it will thank you!

Mary M. Romero

JULY 23

Affirmation: *"Decisiveness is a characteristic of high-performing men and women. Almost any decision is better than no decision at all."*
—Brian Tracy

I don't know that ANY decision is better than no decision at all, but I do appreciate decisiveness. I find decisiveness to be a great quality in working with leaders. The ability to assess the situation, make a pro/con list, and move forward in a timely manner is invaluable. Being stuck between decisions is inefficient and costly, bad for communication, and frustrating to others around you. If decisiveness is a quality you struggle with I encourage you to develop the necessary skills to become more comfortable being able to make swift and timely decisions. You will find that it is frees up your energy for other things if you don't have to keep reconsidering the same issues over and over again. Start with a small easy decision and work your way to bigger decisions. You will gain confidence with every decisive decision you make!

Marcie Wingfield Shanks

JULY 24

Affirmation: *"If you do what you've always done, you'll get what you've always gotten."* —Tony Robbins

Many ambitious people get stuck in the rut of life, repeating behaviors that feel comfortable then wonder why they aren't progressing. In order to make progress, you must get uncomfortable. Getting uncomfortable doesn't mean being reckless. It means deliberately getting outside your comfort zone starting with goal setting.

Goal setting is critical to achieving success in your career. If you aren't setting and working toward those goals, you aren't in control of your destiny.

To achieve optimum success, people must set short and long term goals. In order to set short term goals, you must first consider your long-term aspirations:

1. Where do you see yourself in five years?
2. What type of work do you want to be doing?
3. What type of people do you want to be working with? Working for?
4. From where do you want to be working?
5. How do you want to feel at the end of your work day?

Answering these questions can begin to bring clarity about your long-term professional goals. Once you have thought through these questions, you will determine your course of action.

What do you need to do today to ensure that you will achieve your goals? What do you need to do next week? Next month? Over the next six months? Over the next two years?

If you want a major change in your career, you're going to have to do things differently. In order to break through the cycle of repetition, you're going to have to get uncomfortable. Goal setting and action planning is a safe way to begin making the uncomfortable comfortable so that you can get what you've always wanted.

Jill Johns

JULY 25

Affirmation: *I am calm and relaxed in every situation*

"Someday, everything will make perfect sense. So, for now, laugh at the confusion, smile through the tears and keep reminding yourself that everything happens for a reason." —Paulo Coelho

Life is unpredictable and the unexpected happens. When the situations and circumstances of life are other than ideal, the tendency is to resist what is happening. However, when we resist, we are focusing and putting our energy on what we do not want, and, since what we focus on we create, we are creating more of what we do not want.

The first step to being calm and relaxed in every situation is to accept reality, rather than resist it. Do not waste time and energy denying what is and wishing it wasn't. Instead, accept what is, adjust your perspective to the new reality and then evaluate your choices. Even though reality may not be what you would like it to be, you get to choose how you are going to respond, including your demeanor. When you are calm and relaxed, you are able to make better choices and decisions and you stand in your power.

Janet Christensen

JULY 26

"When people show you who they are, believe them." —Dr. Maya Angelou

If you are a "Pollyanna" or wear "rose-colored glasses," it can set you up to experience pain, betrayal, and even abuse. You must not make excuses for other people's bad behavior. Trust your gut and your intuition when it tells you that something is not right. Trust, but verify. This applies to love relationships, family relationship, and business relationships. Fear of being alone or of losing love and security are powerful deterrents to trusting your own instincts.

However, it is essential that you respect and honor yourself at all times and in all ways. You do not have to accept abusive patterns and unhealthy behavior from the people in your life. You have permission to put yourself first and practice extreme self-care. You are worthy of love and kindness.

Namaste.

Dr. Joanne Siebert, D.C.

JULY 27

Affirmation: *I will love who I see looking back in the mirror no matter my age.*

Haiku: My parking skills, they stink.
The lines, they give me grief.
I need new glasses.

Aging is a fact of life. The body changes, our eyesight weakens, and we have to adjust the way we walk, stand, and generally move through life. Choose to do it with humor. You can't change the inevitable but you can control your reaction to it. Laugh at the adjustments you make to accommodate what doesn't work the way it used to.

Dana D. Cable

JULY 28

Affirmation: *God comforts us so we may be able to comfort others*

Once we get in the presence of God and know His will, we can be a comforter to others when they are going through struggles and challenges.

Cassandra Gaines

JULY 29

If you don't like something, change it. If you can't change it,
change your attitude. —Maya Angelou

If you want different results, you must take different actions. It is easy to complain when your life is heading in an undesirable direction. You can refuse to do anything to change your life or you can take positive action.

Anjanette found herself at a dead end job, underpaid and overworked. She dreaded going to work and while at work, she would complain to anyone that would listen.

Then one day, she realized that complaining was not helping her situation. She actually grew tired of her own talk. She realized nothing will change until she changed. So, she stopped complaining, started looking for a better job and remained focused. When she found a better opportunity; she resigned.

Once Anjanette had a plan in place, she had no interest in complaining because she was doing something about her situation. If you want a different experience, do something about it. Complaining will not help, only positive action will change the course.

Be inspired to silence your complaints and change your attitude.

Affirmation: *I will take the right action to change my life.*

Frenetta Tate

JULY 30

Affirmation: *"I will actively listen to music for ten minutes a day."*

Music can have medicinal effects on each of us. It is a form of art that taps into our inner soul and therefore should be an integral part of our daily lives. Unfortunately, music has become a background noise for many and not something listened to for pure appreciation. We live busy lives and attempt to multitask our time away.

John Lennon said, *"Life is what happens to you when you are busy making other plans."* What have you missed because you were too busy? Music can speak to us in many ways. It can help to soothe the mind, relax the soul, or heal the heart. It can also invigorate and energize. The effects can be different on each person. Do you know what type of music has a positive influence on you?

Spend a minimum of ten minutes each day actively listening to your favorite music. Listen closely to the beat and the melody. What thoughts come to mind? What affect does it have on you?

Judy Singleton

JULY 31

Notes on Life by Nikki Gemmell (extract)

Happy Birthday Sarah C and all others born into this world recently.
I wish you courage.
Not to dim your light among men. Because so many of us,
As women, do.
There's pressure to soften so much: our appetites, wants, spark, our intelligence, our honesty.
Don't ask anyone for permission to be who you are.
You shape your life, no-on else – that is what it means to be a woman today.
I wish you freedom from fear.
Of what other people think of you, of public opinion.
As George Eliot said, "It's never too late to be what you might have been."
Try, and try again.
I wish you wariness of that reducing little word "dependant",
For it means letting ourselves be controlled by another person
and there's a whiny unhealthiness in that.
Dependency doesn't breed contentment.
Never underestimate the power of work –
Accomplishment makes us happy.
I wish courage, at some point, to throw away the map.
An appreciation of failure, a respect for it.
Seeing others strive, fail and strive again spurs us all on,
For we're witnessing the glorious, indomitable human spirit in action.
I wish you the ability to recognize rupture as opportunity.
Embrace the unknown, surrender to it.
Dare.
I wish you bravery.
To be honest. To go against the grain.
To stand up for yourself and for others.
Our lives are made rich by reaching out to those around us,
Not by fencing ourselves in with that little reducing word, 'no'.
There are only two ways to live – as a victim or as
A courageous fighter.
I wish you the blazing latter.
And most fervently, requited love.
A vivid heart. May it never be crushed.
If it is may it love again, fuller, wiser, quieter.

Becky Paroz

AUGUST 1

I get quiet so I can listen.

Sometimes just when I think I have everything in order,
I discover that's not so.

For I get so caught up in the moments and the days with the ups and downs and all around's, that I forget myself.

And. then I unknowingly slide into the should's, the could's, the ought to's and the better -get-it- done -right -now's!

Down I go into that worry and doubt place which slides me into I- am- not- enough and, worse yet, into the I –am- not- worthy place.

Oh, for Heaven's Sake!

I have learned to take a breath or two and get quiet.

But I have to say, crossing back over from the busyness of life into the quiet of Love is a bit daunting, a little scary.

So I have to set myself down, put my hand on my heart, the other on my belly and breathe deep and sweet until I am so quiet I can hear the whispers which remind me so very lovingly,

"God is Love, therefore so am I." (ACIM).

Oh, my.

Thank You.

I remember now.

Sharon McWilliams

AUGUST 2

Affirmation: *"Touched by an angel who brought back my life. Honored me, listened, and look at me when I spoke. Loving, caring, and inspiring. Thank you"*

Every day you wake up you never know who you will meet, what will happen, or even if you win the lottery. It's a new day. Dreams come true. Even in your darkest days things can change in an instant. Keep the faith, be fearless, push forward, and know what you've got somebody wants. Never, never, never give up! Life goes from season to season. Nothing stays the same. Follow no one, but learn from everyone.

Angie Schultz

AUGUST 3

"Today I am aware of my breathing. I promise myself to breathe each breath with awareness."

Nothing is more important than our ability to breathe. Proper breathing allows for maximum inter-change of oxygen and carbon dioxide, maintaining the correct balance of both. The air we breathe sustains us, it nourishes our blood and every cell in the body, breath awareness allows us to focus on the present moment and yet - we pay little or no attention to the way we breathe.

Breath awareness is often dismissed and deemed expendable.

Breathing without awareness limits the mind to creating unhealthy thought pattern, it keeps unhealthy emotions trapped in the body and psyche, and it keeps toxins stuck in the physical body.

Practise breath awareness and enjoy the positive difference it will make!

Gabriela Eikeland

AUGUST 4

Affirmation: *I find the gifts in every situation.*

In <u>every</u> change, challenge and situation there are gifts. Sometimes the gifts are obvious and come prettily packaged, such as winning an all-expense paid trip for two to your dream destination. However, sometimes they are not attractively packaged or obvious and this requires that you be open and actively look for the gifts that emerge. They may be in the kindness of others, or in opportunities to share your strengths, show compassion or make a difference in the life of someone. Sometimes the gifts come disguised in unexpected changes that disrupt life.

Several years ago I received an unexpected phone call from our youngest son, then 23. He got right to the point – he had been diagnosed with cancer and was having surgery the next week. This news rocked both our worlds. The first person I called was my sister-in-law who had experienced breast cancer at 33 and is a success story. Her advice was to look for the gifts as they appeared through the journey, even though I could not see any at the time. This was truly life-transforming advice. An abundance of gifts emerged for all of us over the next several months. One of the most significant was news from the oncologist that the treatment success rate was over 90%. My son lost every hair on his body while undergoing chemotherapy. One day, he showed up wearing a crazy afro wig and we laughed uncontrollably for twenty minutes. This experience brought us closer together, taught us what is truly important in life and to not sweat the small stuff. Today, my son is healthy, happily married with two sons after being told he would not be able to have children.

Gift upon gift.

Janet Christensen

AUGUST 5

I am equipped, encouraged, excited and I am empowered to move on with life. I am looking forward to all the new challenges, opportunities, goodness and life experiences that are yet to come. My past has strengthened and prepared me for my future.

Shirley A. Williams

AUGUST 6

Affirmation: *"Each morning when I awake, I experience again a supreme pleasure - that of being Salvador Dali".* —Salvador Dali

Salvador Dali was a painter, an artist, a womanizer, a drug user, and he had a famous rivalry with Pablo Picasso. He knew he was pretty special before the world discovered his works, and he wasn't afraid to point it out to his audience if he felt they didn't understand.

We all want to belong, be a part of something, be surrounded by friends. The paradox is that we also want to be thought of as special, as unique, as one of a kind.

Stop and take a moment to think about why you have the friends you do, and why they have you as their friend. Ask them why if you don't know. There is something about you that offers to others a benefit. There is a reason, or more than one reason your friends choose to have you in their life. There is something about your friends that make them the friends that you choose to be around. These reasons are the things that make each of you special, unique and exotic to others around you.

Every day when you wake up, remind yourself how wonderful it is that you are you. Love who you are – you are the best person for the job.

Becky Paroz

AUGUST 7

Affirmation: *"In life, we all have to aim; why not aim high? Shoot for the moon. Even if you miss it, you will land among the stars."* —Les Brown

As you focus on your goal or vision, focus on the positive. Like the samurai warrior, commit to your goal with laser precision. Do not lower your guard, it may cost you the battle. Pursue your dream with all your heart with your heart, mind and soul as if your life depended on it. This is the way of the Samurai. The Samurai's word and deed were the same. Honor yourself by keeping your word

Each day take at least one step that will bring your dream to fruition. The journey of a thousand miles begins with one single step. It is your dream, it is worth pursuing and you are the only one that can fulfill it. Do not let your past define your future. It is better to aim and miss than not to aim at all. Every step will bring you closer to your destiny.

Along your journey there may be naysayers and people who would try to sabotage you. When you write your vision on the wall, it will be before you and you can run towards it. Stay on course and do not be led astray.

Surround yourself with positive people who will support and encourage you as you aim high and shoot for the moon!

Lori Tsugawa Whaley

AUGUST 8

Give yourself as much love as you give to others.

Love and support your family and friends unconditionally. Celebrate their joys and lift them up during hard times. Give them the foundation they deserve.

Recognize that you deserve the same amount of love and support that you give to your loved ones. Don't sell yourself short when it comes to appreciating who you are and what you can accomplish.

When you make a mistake, admit it without beating yourself up about it. Take time to analyze where you went wrong and trust that you can avoid the same error the next time.

Take the time to treat yourself to nice things, just like you do with others. Treats to them represent how much you love them. When you treat yourself, you should feel the same kind of love.

Affirmation: *Today, I commit to treating myself as kindly as I treat those I love, because I love and accept myself just the way I am.*

Judith Duclot-Fletcher

AUGUST 9

Watch your thoughts, they become words. Watch your words, they become actions. Watch your actions, they become habits. Watch your habits, they become character. Watch your character, it becomes your destiny.
—Lao Tzu

Affirmation: *"My thoughts spring forth with clarity, purpose and love."*

So much of what we do, feel, accomplish is motivated first by the thoughts we entertain. When our thoughts are motivated with a spirit of love, the actions that follow are also loving, edifying, and healthy and grounded in being vessels of goodwill.

Yet, when we allow our thoughts to turn sour or negative, the resulting actions that spill forth are dark, dangerous, negative, angry, and the list goes on-you get my drift? Fortunately, once we recognize the freeing power of abandoning and not dwelling on negative thoughts, we can move forward with clarity, purpose and love. Daily strive to keep your thoughts pure, kind, loving, forgiving and purposeful.

Let your thoughts be life affirming. Keep your thoughts in line with the highest good of God. Ask the Lord to order your thoughts and steps in His word. Purge you from any unrighteousness; wash away the muck and the mire. May you come forth as pure gold, refined for God's purpose and service. Walk in the destiny God has ordained for your life. Now, claim it done, in Jesus' name.

Betty Patterson Shadrick

AUGUST 10

"Remember, no one can make you feel inferior without your consent."
—Eleanor Roosevelt

You are at peace.

The amount of peace in your life is up to you. You know you can choose to have a peaceful life, so you can consciously make that choice. You may find this to be an enjoyable and successful path through life.

You you are at peace because you make smart decisions each day. Continue making decisions that are congruent with your values and beliefs.

Before you make any decision, examine your values. This will allow you to keep what is most important in the front of your mind. Let go of any urges to stray from this process. Your strong decision-making skills allow will you to be at peace.

Affirmation: *Today, my mind is like a still pond, free of disruption. I feel peace and tranquility and aim to keep it that way.*

Judith Duclot-Fletcher

AUGUST 11

Thoughts are like arrows, once released, they strike their mark. Guard them well, or one day you may be your own victim. —Navajo Proverb

Our thoughts make us who we are. Thinking about others all the time makes us envious and greedy. And, it makes us a victim of our own thoughts because we create the environment. A similar colloquialism, **What we think about we bring about** can be more direct. Our thoughts direct our actions. Bad thoughts create bad actions. Good thoughts can create good actions, but bad thoughts do not create good actions.

Bad thoughts and bad behavior often create bad situations in our lives. A recent study noted that those who believed in **Lucky charms** had more so called luck than those who did not believe in luck. While many who feel lucky also say they work more than others who do not experience luck, the belief in luck whether the item is a lucky golf ball, a rabbits foot, an evil eye, a four leaf clover, or something else, our thoughts make the difference.

The Secret by *Rhonda Byrne*, notes that we attract what we think about. Even the ancient practice of Qigong, notes you should avoid negative words, believing that negativity breeds negativity. The old saying is not failure breeds success; it is success breeds success! In other words, if we have negative thoughts, we bring negative events to us. If think how poor we are, we earn less money than others. When we hang around and talk with folks who are just like us, we experience the same types of things.

Change your thoughts, be direct, and be positive because when they come back to you, you don't want to be hurt. This does not mean don't be realistic. It means recognize the good and the bad, and focus on how to change things for the good!

Katrina Everhart

AUGUST 12

Affirmation: *"All great achievements require time"*. —Maya Angelou

We must be patient when we are trying to accomplish great achievements in life. Patience is a virtue and when we move forward out of timing our plan will not be executed correctly. The plan must be executed correctly and timely. We serve ourselves an in justice when we rush to achieve greatness. Greatness requires strategic planning an analysis while it is in its development stage. Mind mapping, critical thinking and staying focused in addition to acquiring the right resources will help you achieve your goals.

All achievements require time in order to be effective. We must be patient, develop and maintain the plan and stay focused. Great things will happen for you and if you believe you can walk in greatness. Walking in greatness requires action so are you ready to leave the old paradigm and embrace the new. This is your season to take a paradigm shift. Shift into greatness and fulfill purpose because the world is waiting on you to make a difference. Now is your time to fulfill your call and make a difference.

Donna Anderson

AUGUST 13

Affirmation: *"If you can dream it, you can do it"*. —Walt Disney

Jaime was told by her friends that it was impossible for her to fulfill the dream that she was carrying. Jaime realized that she must shut down the voices of her friends that were opposing her dream and she decided to believe in herself that she was capable and competent to achieve her dreams. Jaime realized that she should not have shared her dreams with her friends who tried to discourage her from completing her task. Jaime had the blueprint and decided that she must guard that which was given to her.

Dreams can manifest if you guard and protect what was given to you. Stay away from the dream killers which are people who try to hinder your growth and advancement because of jealousy. Guard your dream and work the structured plan that was given to you. You can and you will fulfill your dream. I speak prosperity and abundance over your life and you shall do great exploits. Be encouraged because every fruitful dream shall come to pass and now you are positioned for the opening of great doors.

Donna Anderson

AUGUST 14

Affirmation: *Did you know that God sends us out so we can bring in others?*

It is a blessing to find our way. It is as much a blessing to help someone find their way. Always look to see who need a hand, a word, a touch, or a shoulder- don't leave anyone in the trenches. God will show you how to love them if you are willing.

Cassandra Gaines

AUGUST 15

Affirmation: *Forgive and Let Go*

Michael Singer, author of the book "The Untethered Soul" is one of my hero's. He was falsely accused of a crime that he did not commit. Instead of feeling revenge and contempt, he instead went to forgiveness and consciously decided to let go. Oprah Winfrey interviewed him and asked how he could possibly do this. He said that he knew the truth. He forgave and let go. It was during these tumultuous years that he wrote his book.

He describes life as a series of events. It's our perceptions, unmet expectations and judgments of these events that make them stressful or painful. If we learn to relax, breathe and release our judgments of these events, our stress levels decrease immensely and we make great strides in our Spiritual journeys, trusting the Divine process.

Our first step in forgiveness is to forgive ourselves. We must forgive ourselves for the stress, fear and upset we've caused ourselves. If we can just "forgive and let go" of the resistances we have and accept life as it comes, we can be much happier and much more available to live the life we are created to live! Be willing to examine your own preconceived notions of how things "should" be. Oprah Winfrey states that forgiveness is giving up the hope that the past could have or should have been any different. What if we just allowed and accepted people as they are instead of trying to mold them into someone we believe they should be? Imagine how relationships could open up! Imagine that relationship with yourself if you completely loved and accepted yourself - ALL of YOURSELF! Relax and release your expectations of yourself. Forgive and Let Go. It is a conscious choice!

Kim Evans

AUGUST 16

Affirmation: *"Good enough never is."* —Debbi Fields

As a competitive and driven person, I am constantly striving for achievement. Many times people ask me who I am competing with. My answer is typically, "No one" to which people typically respond, "Yeah, right!"

Truthfully, I'm not in competition with anyone but I which I realize may be hard to believe. I like to grow. I like to improve. I like to get better. My goal is not to compete with anyone else. If people feel that I am competing with them, then that is their issue. I am simply driven because I don't like complacency. I have high expectations for myself which has led to my success. Good enough is never good enough, right Mrs. Fields?

My lack of complacency has left many in my entourage scratching their heads at times. Why would she leave such a great job? Why would she leave such a great company? Why would she leave her marriage? Why? Why? Why?

The answer to the incessant "whys" over the years has always been very personal. It has never been about anyone else. It's always been about me, as selfish as that may sound. For me, good enough is never good enough. A good enough job isn't good enough. A good enough company isn't good enough. A good enough marriage isn't good enough. I would rather take a risk than stay complacent.

I want better. I want the best for my life. I will continue to pursue more as long as I see fit. I invite you to join me.

Jill Johns

AUGUST 17

Affirmation: *"Celebrate your special birthday"*

This is my birthday! Celebrate your special day the way you want to. I'm a Leo, I love to shine my light and inspire people to find their passion. I love to talk about astrology! Leos are the most generous zodiac of them all. Leos always have issues with their hair. We are the lion, so we talk about our mane a lot. We are not only generous but we are very protective with our family. We are the leaders of the world. Birthdays happen so we can have a day to reflect on our life and value and appreciate ourselves. It's our special day to celebrate our day. We are just like a snowflake, one of a kind. What do you do special on your birthday? Don't wait for someone to do it the way you want to, make your reservations to the restaurant you want to go to or go buy you the bracelet you wanted. Tell your children what you want them to give them. I tell my boys I want a nice note from their heart, and a wrapped gift to me of their choice. I get what I want, and then I'm not disappointed. I ask for what I want. If you have expectations you will probably always be disappointed. Enjoy your birthday and celebrate you! You are here for a reason, so find your purpose and do it with all your heart. Spread the love!

Angie Schultz

AUGUST 18

"Don't think about making women fit the world–think about making the world fit women." —Gloria Steinem

On this day in 1920, the 19th Amendment of the Constitution was ratified and American women won the right to vote. It's amazing to think that Susan B. Anthony and Elizabeth Cady Stanton drafted and introduced the amendment 41 years prior in 1871. Although both women had passed away before they saw their dream realized, there were other suffragists such as Alice Paul, Genevieve Clark, and others who picked up their torch and carried it across the finish line.

As a woman who considers herself a feminist, I ask the question: what torch are you bearing to continue progress for women's rights? Perhaps your task is far less noteworthy than fighting for voting rights for women, but nonetheless, important. What are you doing to mentor and empower other young women? Provide support for women's causes? Or maybe you're just letting your voice be heard when it comes to injustices.

Even in 2014, men earn higher salaries for the same amount of work and far outnumber women in positions of power in all industries. Even more troubling is the fact that sexual assault against women is still a prominent problem in the world. Yes, women have come a long way since 1920. But there's a long way yet to go. Take an active role in helping to make a difference in this journey of progress.

Dawn Jamison

AUGUST 19

"Discipline is just choosing between what you want now and what you want most." —Unknown

Karen wanted to lose weight.

She had tried many, many times before, but it never worked. She loved her Mountain Dew and fast food too much. Of course, those weren't the only things she loved, but they were certainly the most obvious things contributing to her weight problem.

One day she decided that she didn't want to be fat anymore. She decided she wanted to be fit and healthy so she could be more active with her two sons. First, she gave up fast food. It felt like someone had taken away her best friend. She grieved the loss of her companion. She started cooking her meals at home. She even changed her route home from work so she didn't have to drive past any fast food restaurants; a daunting task given the prevalent availability of these types of establishments.

Twenty pounds lost.

She gave up Mountain Dew. She had been slowly decreasing her consumption, but she stopped drinking it completely and began drinking water, which she hated. Another best friend lost. More grieving. Eventually the water began to taste good and her thirsty cells thrived with hydration.

Ten pounds lost.

She began exercising. At a gym. 4 days a week. She never thought that would happen. And she actually started enjoying it and looking forward to it after a while.

Twelve more pounds.

The journey continues and what she wants is in sight. Self-love and self-acceptance are not because of the weight loss. Self-love and self-acceptance are because she honored herself.

Dr. Joanne Siebert, D.C.

AUGUST 20

Affirmation: *"I would rather die of thirst, than drink from the cup of mediocrity."* —Anonymous

I am driven. To succeed, to challenge, to achieve, to reach further – these words inspire me to get out of bed every day and make a difference in my life, and the lives of those around me.

Sometimes I am driven insane. The violence, the horror perpetuated through cycles of abuse, the outcry from those who have nothing, watching those who have everything throw it away.

How do I make a difference through the clamour of the life that surrounds me? By making everything I do and am involved in, the best that I can. By reminding myself, that through exceptional action, I may inspire, motivate and challenge those around me to step up – to be better, give more, try harder, aim higher.

I want this world to be the best that it can for our future generations. I want the leaders from hundreds of years from now to look at this point in history and say – that was the turning point. That is where the human race decided to aim high, instead of accept average. Where everyone said "Enough! We will not accept second best behaviour from our leaders or ourselves from now, or ever again!"

And it starts with me, every day, as I start each day, setting my standards to high, and refusing the easy, readily available average and mediocre that surrounds me.

I would rather die of thirst than drink from that cup.

Becky Paroz

AUGUST 21

Affirmation: *"I treasure the gifts in my life, big and small."*

It is so easy to take things for granted, especially when they've been present in your life for a long time. Your family, friends, freedom, health, safety, the availability of what you need to survive, modes of transportation, nature, and so much more. To truly treasure all of the gifts in your life requires keen awareness and deep appreciation. It goes beyond gratitude to the place inside where your heart is full with the realization of how truly fortunate you are. It often takes losing something before you truly appreciate what you had. Take action before that happens in your life.

Make a list of 10 things, big and small, that you treasure in your life. Review it and add to it regularly. If there are people on your list, tell them often that you treasure them.

Michelle Richardson

AUGUST 22

Affirmation: *The best and most beautiful things in the world cannot be seen or even touched - they must be felt with the heart.* —Helen Keller

When have you been in the presence of someone you adored and spoke not a word. Love is the kindness that is felt within your heart.

I am reminded of my beloved rescued pet Teddy who has been blind since birth. He cannot see me, his adoptive rescue "sister" Gracie from Puerto Rico, or his home along the Ohio River. But this little guy knows he is loved beyond words.

Think of those you love and hold them in your heart even if they are far away. Love knows no boundaries.

Linda Ellis Eastman

AUGUST 23

Affirmation: *"You must do the things you think you cannot do".*
—Eleanor Roosevelt

Denise had an inferiority complex because she has failed several times at a task and she believed that she may never overcome that fear. Denise felt she could never accomplish this task because she had tried several times before and she was always disappointed because she could not accomplish that which was given to her. Denise decided to empower herself and combat her fear by trying again to accomplish the task that constantly defeated her. Through she toiled and struggled in her mind she decided to believe in spite of the odds against her that she could accomplish this task.

Denise decided not to be held captive to her thoughts and her failures any longer. Denise pressed and continued to pursue against the odds by any means necessary. You must continue to pursue and advance in spite of the odds against you. You must do the things you cannot do cities, countries and nations may be impacted and changed do to your new discovery. You are strong and you can do it. Failure is captured and defeated so you must now walk in victory.

Donna Anderson

AUGUST 24

"I do not wish [women] to have power over men; but over themselves."
—Mary Wollstonecraft

Change is in your future.

You are walking away from things that makes you feel less than who you are today.

Your future beckons you to make a change for the better. To move beyond your past, you treat your future as a clean slate and use the wisdom of experience as a compass for decision-making.

You have reached an epiphany that is calling for change and rejuvenation. Your soul hums with the sound of yearning and re-growth.

You are ready for the exciting changes that I know are coming. You are so confident that you can do anything you set your heart to do. Your mind, body, and soul are in sync with your goals for change and nothing can hinder your desires.

If you face an outside challenge, remove it from your path. Your will is stronger than any factor you may encounter on your journey to the new you. With challenge comes strength that is earned through experience.

Making changes in your life opens new doors for you. You have the power to create happiness through the power of positive thinking.

Affirmation: *Today, I choose to change my future in a way that sets me above my previous notions about who I am. I move beyond my past to make small changes each day.*

Judith Duclot- Fletcher

AUGUST 25

Affirmation: *"As a rock star, I have two instincts, I want to have fun, and I want to change the world. I have a chance to do both."* —Bono

As a woman, I have two instincts: I want to take care of others and I want to take care of myself. I, like Bono, have a chance to do both.

I take care of others by helping them on their journey to growth, improvement and fulfillment. I provide training, coaching and resources that help women identify their goals. I hold them accountable and able. I show them love, support and belief in their ability and their potential.

I take care of myself by learning and growing which allows me to inspire others. I attend conferences, read books, listen to podcasts and communicate with as many thought leaders as possible in order to stretch myself. I incorporate the things I learn into my daily life, ensuring that I practice what I preach.

The good news for me is that both of these things ultimately allow me to have fun and change the world, just like Bono. I have met many amazing people on my journey. I have learned from many masters. I have encountered countless women on a quest similar to mine – hungry to help others while simultaneously enriching their own experience.

What two instincts do you have? What are you doing today to make them happen?

Jill Johns

AUGUST 26

Affirmation: *I will be clear in all of my communications.*

Haiku: To post, or not to
          post, that is the question. What
          the heck, I'm posting.

If you have something to say – say it clearly, concisely, consciously, with firm commitment. If it can positively affect the lives of others, then say it. Keep it short, keep it relevant, and keep it positive.

Dana D. Cable

AUGUST 27

*"Every time you are tempted to react in the same old way,
ask if you want to be a prisoner of the past or a pioneer of the future."*
—Dr. Deepak Chopra

In every moment, we have a choice. Am I a prisoner of the past or a pioneer of my future? While the prisoner is tempting and very known to us, it won't give us anything more than the experiences already filling our lives. The same old reaction yields the same old outcome.

To create newly is to step beyond what we've known so that we may have a rich, new experience aligned with our Highest Good. We are being called to be the pioneers in our lives, planting new seeds in soils of opportunity and growth.

To be a pioneer, be willing to try on a new way of being. Be open to addressing a situation from your Inner Wise Self. Ask her what she would do in this moment. How would she address this person? What choice would she make? What other possibilities does she see that you may not?

Your Inner Wise Self is there to live out your soul's calling. Partner with her and you will never be a prisoner again.

Paula Onysko

AUGUST 28

Affirmation: *"Respond instead of React".* —Gary Zuchov

Wow! What a powerful distinction. As Gary reminds us, the Universe will give us plenty of stimuli to which we will want to react. He teaches that we will know that we've progressed Spiritually when we can experience our feelings and emotions and consciously choose to respond instead of react. Wouldn't the world be a better place if we each did this? Think of the Wars that could have been/will be prevented when we learn to respond instead of react. I often follow the wise words of the late Martha Moore Stevens. She would feel the upset or anger, allow it to come through and pass, then finally say, "Thank you God for letting me get rid of that little impurity!"

The next time your spouse or your children push your buttons, take a breath, relax and intentionally decide to respond instead of react. You will be amazed at how much calmer and happier your home will be.

Kim Evans

AUGUST 29

Affirmation: *"We are what we repeatedly do. Excellence then is not an act, but a habit."* —Aristotle

In today's busy world it is so easy to get caught up in the hustle and bustle of life that often diligence, and determination fall to the way side. It is important to have priorities that determine where your focus will be and that guide what you repeatedly do. In our culture time-starved culture we feel as if we never have enough time. Is that really the truth, or do we just put too much time and emphasis on things that aren't truly important?

What are you doing repeatedly with your time that you know you could put to better use? Is it a television show, a game, or an activity that will have no meaning in 5, 10, or 15 years? What is holding you back from repeatedly doing something that will create excellence in your life? Take one small step today to weed out something unimportant and make room for something that is truly meaningful to you. Maybe it's more time with your kids, friends, or family. Perhaps it's making time to take care of your body with exercise, or a hobby you've previously given up. Whatever it is – you deserve excellence in your life. Make time for it repeatedly.

Marcie Wingfield Shanks

AUGUST 30

Affirmation: *'You have not lived a perfect day unless you've done something for someone who will never be able to repay you."* —Ruth Smeltzer

Something wonderful happens when you connect and extend your hand to someone in need; someone who will not be able to repay you. This act of kindness nourishes the soul of both the giver and recipient because we are all connected.

When my Mother and I traveled to the San Francisco, discovering the perfect restaurant was one of our highlights. We dined at a wonderful establishment and enjoyed a fabulous dinner. Our eyes were larger than our stomachs, and the waiter packaged our food. As we walked to our hotel, we noticed a disheveled man sitting on a step with his head hung low. We gladly offered him our food and wished him well. The next day, we walked near the restaurant and was warmly greeted by the same man looking transformed! He shared that if two lovely women cared about him, then he was going to start caring about himself. We were the ones that were blessed and touched!

In 2000, the movie «Pay it Forward» a young boy attempts to make the world a better place by helping three people. In turn, those three people would help three more people by paying it forward with acts of kindness. The movie has a positive effect on its audience and it encouraged people to look for ways to share kindness and to think beyond themselves even to this day.

When you care for someone who will not be able to repay you, you are helping the world and all of mankind.

Lori Tsugawa Whaley

AUGUST 31

Affirmation: *I believe in myself.*

In order to live with purpose, passion and realize your potential, it is vital that you have an unbending belief in yourself and your abilities. This is not the same as being egotistical. Rather, this involves you acknowleging, accepting, developing, appreciating and being willing to share and express your gifts and talents. When you believe in yourself, you consistently expand your horizons through learning and moving outside of your comfort zone. You wholeheartedly believe that what you put your mind to, you will achieve.

You are the one and only unique you, well worth believing in.

Janet Christensen

SEPTEMBER 1

"If you want to know a thing, read that. If you want to understand a thing, study that. And if you want to master a thing, teach that."
—Yogi Bhajan

I am a teacher. There are many things that I have been educated and trained to teach, but instead of just sticking to those subjects I have a habit of teaching the very thing that I need to learn the most. I used to think it was self-centered, but now I know otherwise.

It is wise to teach what you do not know in order to master it! In the teaching of a subject, we are knowledgeable because we have read *it* and we have studied *it*. And in our preparation to teach others we not only receive the blessing of helping others learn, but we also receive the knowledge that makes us masters of the subject. Why wouldn't we want to teach a thing in order to master a thing? Go out, be brave and teach.

Kymberley Clemons Jones

SEPTEMBER 2

"Two things define you. Your patience when you have nothing and your attitude when you have everything." —Raw For Beauty (Internet)

Never lose sight of where you came from, the people who helped you along the way, or the bridges you had to cross to get there. If you do, it only makes it a more unpleasant trip if you find yourself back there. You could find it to be an unbearable endeavor when you attempted to cross over the bridges you may have destroyed along the way.

Shirley A. Williams

SEPTEMBER 3

"Today I allow my authentic self to shine. "

One of the most important steps in recognising your own authentic self and to give yourself a chance to develop your highest self and potential is to know, and to honor, your personal core values and needs.

Respecting your values and your needs means that you are in alignment with your true self, and if who you are is in alignment with what you do, you will be able to embrace your authentic self and you will be the wonderful person that you are meant to be.

Having discovered your authentic self will set you free from need for approval and self-sabotage. Start your journey to being your authentic self and BE a woman in your own right!

Gabriela Eikeland

SEPTEMBER 4

Affirmation: *"Change happens when you understand what you want to change so deeply that there is no reason to do anything but act in your own best interest."* —Geneen Roth

Every day we complain about the changes we want to see in our lives. If you want change, a different life, to pursue a passion, dream, or goal – you have to know it intimately. You have to know to your core why you want it, what you are and aren't willing to give up to achieve it, and what it will mean to you when you arrive at the destination. Without this intimacy with our deepest desires, change will stagnate and become an unachievable pursuit. What are you longing to change in your life? Do you know it intimately? What steps can you take to make it in your own best interest to change?

Marcie Wingfield Shanks

SEPTEMBER 5

Affirmation: *I will remember those who paved the way for me.*

Haiku: My ancestors farmed,
              My people, my heritage.
              I love what they sowed.

Carry on the traditions that were passed down through your ancestors. Remember and honor what they worked for, stood for, and the memories they created. Take the opportunity to create your own traditions to be carried on by your followers, be they children, grandchildren, co-workers, or community.

Dana D. Cable

SEPTEMBER 6

Affirmation: *I know that it's okay to indulge now and then.*

Haiku: Thanks to Godiva,
               Being bad with chocolate,
               I don't regret it.

The body is a temple to be honored and well-maintained. However, life is too short not to celebrate. Don't let your scale dictate your life. Grab a piece of chocolate – or whatever is your favorite "poison" – and enjoy.

Dana D. Cable

SEPTEMBER 7

Affirmation: *Don't worry about everything*

Does worry help you pay bills? Does worry make you feel good? Does worry make you sick? Worry comes from the gut. That's when you know you've worried too much. Where does faith come into the picture? Do you have faith? Why worry then? Does it help the problem? Does it make you more balanced when you worry? What are some ways to move forward and have the faith?

1. Believe in yourself that you have all the answers you need inside.
2. Have and keep the faith
3. Be accountable to the problem and take care of it yourself. Don't count on anyone else.
4. Be spontaneous

As you work through your worry and change the habit of doing it, you might see how it DOESN'T benefit you. It takes you out of the moment, sucks your energy and you're not productive in your daily living. Worry makes you tired, puts you in a bad mood, affects other people when its not their problem and you're not any fun to be around. It changes your attitude. It's bad energy. Is that how you want to be portrayed? Lets face it, it's a very bad habit and it doesn't work. Get to know how you work and who you are. Everyone is different and we all work through things in our own unique way. Your past is your past. Learn from it, make better choices and help yourself by not worrying, so you can be a more whole and better person.

STOP THE WORRY!

Worry does nothing good for you. Changing your words will change your life. Start working that muscle you have never tapped into. By not worrying you can start engaging in being a better friend, mother, spouse. Calm yourself and know that everything will work out just the way it was supposed to. There are no mistakes. Your destiny is already set. Enjoy the ride. Try something new and have fun with it. Make it a game. When you think that you have worked hard at not worrying and replaced it with optimism and faith, go treat yourself, and value yourself for wanting to be better. You deserve it.

HAPPY BIRTHDAY TO MY SON, BORN ON THIS DAY!

Angie Schultz

SEPTEMBER 8

Affirmation: *"Be genuine....no one likes a fake! It's like the difference between a cubic zirconia and a diamond...those who can tell the difference....will."*

Have you reached the point in your life where you are actually living your true, authentic self? When you receive a gift say, a piece of jewelry. There are times when you can just tell it is 'not the real thing'. Not that this is a 'bad thing' all the time but, when you were truly hoping for something special....something amazing, and something so unique it touches your heart and soul, you are looking for the 'real deal'. This is what the people you come into contact with are looking for as well. They don't want someone who pretends to be something they are not. Being genuine and authentic takes courage, strength, and self-assurance which the 'fakes' lack. The people who matter to you in your life will know the difference if you are simply *acting* like a trustworthy, reliable, and genuine person or, if your true spirit shines bright with all these facets for all to see!

You decide....are you a cubic or a natural gem!

Mary M. Romero

SEPTEMBER 9

Affirmation: *"Holding onto past hurts and pains only saps our own energy to be at our full potential. Is there something you can let go of today to give yourself the gift of inner peace?"*

We have all come from a place where there are past experiences that have brought us pain, unhappiness, disappointment, fear, and the list goes on. Yet, by holding onto these past hurts and pains only saps our own energy so that we are not able to be at our full magnificent potential that we are meant to be. We must start, one day at a time, one event at a time, to let go and let our true inner beauty be shown to the world… not what others or events would have us define ourselves as. Everyone is entitled to his/her own opinion. But, the one that matters most is the one you have when you are staring back at yourself in the mirror.

Start today! Today is the beginning of a new way of defining yourself. Pick one….just one old piece of baggage that you can let go of today, *forever*, to give yourself the gift of inner peace. You will be amazed at the room you make by letting go, for something far more fulfilling in your life. Be your own best friend and continue your journey with a new perspective every day!

Mary M. Romero

SEPTEMBER 10

"Everybody is a genius. But if you judge a fish on its ability to climb a tree,
it will live its whole life believing that it is stupid." —Albert Einstein

I know a boy
who can't read that well.
His games and his toys
are labeled distraction.

He is told that dyslexia
is a gift to embrace.
But he wishes sincerely
that he fit in this place.

But, really his secret is
that he is smart.
He just doesn't learn
the way others purport .

Imagination runs wild
and ideas flow freely.
If only this child
could take tests as easily.

Joys and frustration
sprinkle his days.
Laughter or tears
can come when he's praised.

I hope that one day
he can see the truth.
That the way that he is
is part of his youth.

The world needs his gift
more than he can imagine.
One day the doubters
will wonder what happened.

Dr. Joanne Siebert, D.C.

SEPTEMBER 11

What is life? It is the flash of a firefly in the night. It is the breath of a buffalo in the wintertime. It is the little shadow which runs across the grass and loses itself in the sunset. —Blackfoot Proverb

As we mourn for all the lives lost on 9-11, remember to live your life to the fullest. Don't be afraid of the past, move forward into the future. And, think about ways to make your life and community better today and tomorrow. Try practicing at least one act of random kindness today as you never know what tomorrow brings.

Katrina Everhart

SEPTEMBER 12

"You don't have to be anti-man to be pro-woman." —Jane Galvin Lewis

An abundant future awaits You!

Today's successes are the icing on your cake of abundance! Get excited when you open your eyes each morning because you know great things await you. You are a blessed child whose story is to achieve all you set your sights on.

Life's obstacles are only temporary roadblocks, so avoid letting them change your resolve and focus. Use your talents and abilities to find a way around each challenge so you can continue on the path to success.

There is nothing to stop you from reaching the pinnacle in both your personal and professional exploits.

On days when it might tire, allow yourself to rest. Recognize that rest is an essential element to building your endurance.

You know an abundant future awaits you because you see every situation as an opportunity to do or achieve something great. Embrace even the most understated opportunity and try to find the worth in it.

When you figure that even if an experience yields results other than what you expect, it can teach you which path to take the next time around.

Affirmation: *Today, I avoid wasting my time worrying about what I have yet to accomplish. I remind myself of what I already have under my belt and use those achievements to propel my drive. I live without regret because every experience serves a purpose.*

Judith Duclot-Fletcher

SEPTEMBER 13

Affirmation: *"Resist your fear; fear will never lead to you a positive end. Go for your faith and what you believe"*. —T.D. Jakes

In a boxing match there are two opponents and the strongest opponent is usually the winner. Each opponent is skillful however the opponent who strategizes and assesses his opponent's weakness will win because they have mastered the art. The opponent who wins must be fearless regardless of what he sees in front of him.

Fear is the opponent of faith and it can ultimately destroy you if you succumb to it. Faith gives you that power to oversee all obstacles and hindrances. Faith makes you fearless if you believe that you can accomplish what you believe. Faith overcomes all barriers and hindrances and it destroys the element of fear. It is time to walk in faith if you believe it you can receive it. Place faith on your obstacles, situations, hurts and pain because it may lead you to a positive end.

Donna Anderson

SEPTEMBER 14

Affirmation: *I am grateful for all that I have.*

"There is a calmness to a life lived in gratitude, a quiet joy."
—Ralph H. Blum

Today, you are invited to gift yourself with a gratitude stone. This could be a small stone from your garden or a semi-precious stone such as a piece of quartz, agate, tiger's eye, or whatever else captures your fancy. When you choose your stone, hold it, connect with it, and make sure that it resonates with you.

Carry your gratitude stone with you in your pocket or purse. Every time you touch your gratitude stone, it anchors a thought of gratitude and reminds you to take a moment to appreciate someone or something already in your life, or that you would like to have in your life. You may be grateful for anything - your job or business, your family, your health, your friends, your home, the good weather, or whatever else that comes to mind that makes you happy and grateful.

Whenever you find yourself feeling overwhelmed, hold your gratitude stone and you can immediately access this positive energy of gratitude and put yourself in the right state and frame of mind.

Each thought of gratitude is a magnet and serves as an energy spark to the Universe. Every aspect of our lives grows richer as we give thanks for what we have, and what is yet to come. Keep your gratitude flowing and be open to receive. The Universe will help you with the rest.

Janet Christensen

SEPTEMBER 15

Affirmation: *I am human, not perfect, but always evolving toward excellence.*

Haiku   Superior brain,
Does not include common sense,
I am still – human.
We all make mistakes. None of us have all the answers. It's okay.
Life goes on – and so will you.

Dana D. Cable

SEPTEMBER 16

Affirmation: *What we have once enjoyed, we can never lose. All that we have loved deeply becomes a part of us.* —Helen Keller

Remember all the past loves of your life. No matter whether they are alive or deceased, they have become a part of you forever.

Linda Ellis Eastman

SEPTEMBER 17

Affirmation: *A book is the only place in which you can examine a fragile thought without breaking it, or explore an explosive idea without fear it will go off in your face. It is one of the few havens remaining where a person's mind can get both provocation and privacy.* —Edward P. Morgan

While you may not be able to travel to exotic world places or to engage in first hand encounters in order to explore a foreign culture, you can pick up a book and read about anything you desire. Books are a gift ready for the taking. Reading gives you the tools to explore life and to experience new adventures. It helps to increase your vocabulary and gives you the confidence and self esteem to engage in a variety of conversations. Reading can provide an escape from daily concerns, it can help people relax and can it can provide an avenue for socialization especially if you wish to join a group and discuss a particular book with colleagues.

Technology has shown a slow but dangerous pace in terms of replacing books and reading. I urge you not to ever let reading books slip from your life. Become engaged in the world around you through every sensory means that you can. Books will never let you down and they are always available. Honest, books are my best friends. After all, they are loyal, they don't argue back and you can shut them down and close the book whenever you want!

Barbara J. Bowes, CHRP, CMC, CCP, M.Ed.

SEPTEMBER 18

Affirmation: *"You don't have to take back what you don't say!"*
—David Evans

These wise words by my husband have served me well. When my emotions get the best of me and I am tempted to unload all my feelings and frustrations on some poor unsuspecting soul, I remember his words. This allows me to stop, breath and take a moment to really think about what I'm about to say. Thinking before we speak allows us to glimpse the impact our words may have on the person with which we are conversing. That momentary insight may inspire us to change our thoughts and choose again what to say.

Today, think before you speak. Let your first comments be complimentary for the other person. Start with gratitude for the situation regardless of what it is. Be grateful for the experience. When you begin your speaking from appreciation, love and gratitude, powerful moments ensue that affirm you and everyone around you!

Kim Evans

SEPTEMBER 19

I celebrate with retreat!

I must admit that when summer comes to an end, I feel a wistfulness, a little melancholy at the fact that I must wear shoes again. I must get out my sweaters and jackets, and later coats and scarves and gloves---my many pairs of gloves so when I lose one or two, more are around somewhere waiting for my hands, thank goodness!

I guess the child in me loves summer so as it's such a time for my free spirit to play outdoors all the time, spending time with the warm breezes and the soft green carpet under my feet. I remember to make clover chains for necklaces and flower crowns as I inhale the soft yellow of the dandelions, and make rings of violets for my fingers.

I love my big swing by the creek and the springhouse in the shade on a really hot, humid day. I choose to even forego the air conditioning inside.

I love sitting in my mama's rocker on the kitchen deck at night counting all the stars and enjoying the fireflies lighting up all the trees surrounding my home.

Well, it's time to count all those many blessings as summer passes! Time to celebrate with a little retreat moment, lighting a candle for the beauty of this transition moment right before Mother Nature slides into autumn with all her glorious reds and oranges and golds and purples!

Ah, Fall…I can do this! Let me go get my sweater, my hiking boots and my retreat bag! Time to celebrate this beautiful autumn!

Sharon McWilliams

SEPTEMBER 20

Affirmation: *"We must have good domestic relations with ourselves before we can have good foreign relations with others."*
—Rabbi Joshua Lothliebman

My high school class graduation song was "Let there be peace on earth and let it begin with me.» This is a powerful and profound statement that rings true today. Peace does begin with the individual and I did not fully understand it until later in life.

A good domestic relation with yourself is vital and a prerequisite to good foreign relations with others. We speak well of others; we can also speak well of ourselves. Develop your inner qualities and appreciate your own uniqueness. Take an inventory and list all of your positive traits. This list could include:

Compassionate, tenacious, enterprising, intelligent, honest, trustworthy; and the list is limitless!

Why spend time and energy on negative self talk? You are so much more than your negative traits. A loving thing you can do for others is to love yourself first. When you love yourself, you will have more harmonious relationships with others. When you spend your time loving others, you will not have time to be at odds with them.

Today, spend time on yourself, inventory your positive traits and make it a great day!

Lori Tsugawa Whaley

SEPTEMBER 21

Affirmation: *I've learned that people will forget what you said, and people will forget what you did, but people will never forget how you made them feel.* —Maya Angelou

My motto is to always make the person you meet or see feel a little bit better then when you first met them. So when you walk away you know in your heart you know you made that person feel a little better then when you started talking. It's a great feeling. You become a good listener (if you want to) you look at the person when they talk. Be kind to someone who seems mad; hold a door open for an older person, or for a mom and her kids. Write your mom a nice note, and thank her for her time. It's always about the little things that count. Be what you want other people to do for you. Be the inspiration, find your passion, and be happy right where you are, even if the circumstances aren't great. Choose yes to stay in a great attitude. People love to be around others who don't complain and keep their attitude intact. Be one of those people!

Angie Schultz

SEPTEMBER 22

We can only change ourselves.

We used to ask my Grandpa why he smoked a pipe because it's so bad for him. He always had the same reply: "Why do you eat candy? It's bad for you." Hmmm…we didn't quite know how to answer that one! Well, as it happened, we never stopped eating candy, and he never stopped smoking his pipe. As much as we wanted him to quit, he wouldn't change. And neither did we.

I think of that story when I observe someone's behaviors that I would like to see change. The reality is we can never change someone else. They must first choose to change, and then act on that choice. All we can do is try to influence them, whether or not it has the desired end-result.

But how do we influence others? We know that actions speak louder than words. I was still young when my grandpa passed away, so I don't have the opportunity today to influence his behaviors. But what I can see now is that if I was not willing to quit eating candy, how could I expect him to quit his pipe? I could have started to influence his behavior by choosing to change my behavior. Yes, even when I was 8 years old!

To influence change in others, we must start with ourselves.

Rebecca Sheperd

SEPTEMBER 23

Affirmation: *"Nothing is impossible, the word itself says 'I'm possible'."*
—Audrey Hepburn

Whatever we dream of is possible. Just the fact that it manifested into our conscious thoughts means that it is a reachable goal.

That being said, the journey toward your dream can often be challenging. We must weave first through our own doubts and fears and then deal with the naysayers.

By working through those obstacles and keeping your eye on your goal, it gives your life meaning plus a thrilling sense of purpose and often adventure.

Remember that the possibilities are endless and that all great outcomes started with a single idea.

Identify your goal and write it down. Contemplate possible steps toward reaching this vision and act on one small step today, knowing that it is bringing you closer to your dream.

Maritza Rodriguez-Arseneau

SEPTEMBER 24

When you face fear, it faces you.
You have a heart, spirit, mind and full body at your disposal.
What does fear have? A story at best.

If you have lived, you have felt fear at some point. It can pull your stomach in knots, create tightness in your chest or paralyze you from your next step.

But what really is fear? It is a story that lives only in your mind. It is no more real than a happy fairy tale you could choose to tell.

Face your fear. "Oh hello there fear."

And get specific about what you fear and the meaning you are giving it.

"I fear X. If X happens, that means _____."

Acknowledge this fear for what it is – one possible outcome. But remember what you have inside you. You have the world's resources, energy and love to draw on.

The best way to set a fear free is to go about your day doing one thing that proves the fear wrong. Because once you do, the mind say, "Oh, I can't have that fear anymore. I just proved its opposite."

Fear isn't bad. It's the inner child protecting you. She wants to know that you are safe. So invite her to see that right here and now, you are. Safety comes in trusting yourself and life to provide, which it does in abundance.

Paula Onysko

SEPTEMBER 25

Affirmation: *"Rule 101: If you're a man, and you still think a woman can't compete with you, she's about to blindside you, pal"*. —George Lois

George Lois was one of the original "Mad Men", not from the TV series, from the real-life group that inspired the series. He used to be one of those men that sold vacuum cleaners to women, by making them believe that they could only be a 'real' woman, with whatever brand they were selling at the time. Nothing much has changed in a lot of the advertising we are subjected to today, but George Lois obviously has.

When we women refuse to buy into the rules – that competition is not for ladies, that you can't get to the board room unless you sleep your way there, that you will never be as good as a man – you blindside the people around you.

Challenge the belief that you can't compete. After all, my experience shows me that when women compete, they can be collaborative, encouraging everyone in the belief that as you all compete, you all grow and become better – better skilled, better experience, better at whatever you are competing in.

When women compete, every body can win. I believe that is something that we can teach men, that while there might be a "winner" and a "loser", everybody still takes something from the experience, in which case, everybody "wins".

And if you do have one of these men in your life, feel free to blindside him with your brilliance.

Becky Paroz

SEPTEMBER 26

"We need to be more selective about the commitments we undertake and to realize that saying no to some allows us to concentrate more fully on those we say yes to." —Eric V. Copage

Affirmation: *"Today we look closely and seriously on the WHY of busyness."*

Have you said YES once too often and now are faced with the serious need to assess why you embrace busyness? Time is precious; you need to set boundaries where you can give the best, uncompromised service. Why do you sometimes feel like a crazed banshee; lacking direction, personal fulfillment, order, purpose or direction?

Why have you become a slave to being BUSY? Is there a need to appear busy, so others will think more highly of you, however short lived? Are you using your talents and gifts in the best way to influence long-term positive and life sustaining actions and results for yourself and others? How do you reined in the craziness to gain greater clarity from your Savior and Lord and to hear His will for your life?

To be honest, I may not have all the answers. I'm still striving to set boundaries that free me to be the best I can be while stilling the clamoring noise /raging storm within. Nonetheless, let's start this process together. We'll get sufficient rest, read God's word, pray, meditate, exercise, and embrace solitude to clearly hear God's instructions. We'll cease taking on too many responsibilities, release unnecessary and unwanted commitments, and become wiser stewards of our time. We'll selectively and prayerfully choose activities to embrace with fervor, compassion, and strength. Today we walk the path that ultimately leads to greater productivity for God. We take those steps now and continually seek God's wisdom to show us the way.

Betty Patterson Shadrick

SEPTEMBER 27

Affirmation: *I joyfully release what frees me to move forward.*

"Close some doors. Not because of pride, incapacity or arrogance, but simply because they no longer lead somewhere." —Paulo Coelho

Is there a belief, object or relationship in your life that you are holding onto that is keeping you stuck and preventing you from creating what you desire? What is the one thing, relationship or way of thinking that, if you were to release it, would free you to move forward?

When you are able to identify whatever your one thing is and release it, you set in motion powerful influences over what you manifest in your life. The act of releasing it, creates a void, or vacuum. Since nature abhors a vacuum, your subconscious mind, higher self and the Universe will work together to try and fill the void. Therefore, it is vital that you consciously choose what you want to have fill the vacuum you have created.

What new belief, object or relationship do you want to embrace to move you forward to create the life you want to have?

You choose what to release and you choose what to embrace. Truly empowering.

Janet Christensen

SEPTEMBER 28

"Anticipate the good so that you may enjoy it." —Ethiopian proverb

Affirmation: *When you praise God, you create an atmosphere to receive His blessings.*

On this Sabbath day, praise God for His greatness, loving kindness, provision, and protection. Praise God who holds you in the palm of His hands, knows all about you and yet still loves, despite your failures and frailties.

Praise God for the periods of chastening and correcting, those periods where you were stretched beyond what you thought was capable; yet periods that were necessary to refine and refashion you for greater service and productivity.

Praise God that He provides all your needs and is bountiful in blessings. Praise Him for good health, for the life force that flows in your body, for healing, restoration and His abiding love and strength for today and tomorrow.

Praise God for sending the very special people or angels in your life who genuinely care, offer concern, support, sound advice and counsel. Praise your Father for never, ever leaving or forsaking you, for hiding you under the shadow of His mighty hands.

Praise God for victory over sin, for turning away from past negative actions and behaviors. When you're weak, lost your way, God is still there, still hears your pleading cries and answers with compassion and redemption.

Affirm you could not and would not want to make this journey without Him by your side. Bless the name of the Lord, Bless your Savior, Bless your all and all!

Betty Patterson Shadrick

SEPTEMBER 29

Affirmation: *"Setting goals is the first step in turning the invisible into the visible."* —Tony Robbins

By June 2023, my husband and I will be free. If all goes well, our youngest child will graduate from high school in May 2023 which means that by June 2023, we will be free.

Let me define free: free, for us, is the ability to go anywhere and do anything that we would like to do in that moment. If we want to live on a sailboat, we are free to do it. If we want to travel to the National Parks for a few months, we are free to do it. If we want to continue working in our jobs, we are free to do it. Free means flexibility. Free means navigating life from the driver's seat. Free means pure, authentic decision-making capability. Free means that we don't have any major bills or financial obligations holding us back from living our dreams.

Having this goal of freedom has done two things for our relationship: it has created a sense of common purpose and it allows us to have a framework for our decision-making process. Our common purpose is that we both want to experience this level of freedom and this goal has given us direction and vision. Just as corporations plan strategically for the future, so do we as a couple. Our goal has solidified our decision-making framework allowing us to determine if our choices are taking us closer to or further from our goal.

What goals have you set?

There will be bumps along the way. We may change our mind. But for now, having this goal has turned our life dreams from invisible to visible. I'm looking forward to crossing the finish line.

Jill Johns

SEPTEMBER 30

Affirmation: *Passion might be what got you into trouble at work and at home but it is lighting your way toward a new career based on natural talent. Seek it out.*

Many of us have heard that old standard career guidance phrase, "find your passion and you'll find your job!" The problem is that no-one really teaches us how to find our passion. In fact, in most cases, we trip over our passion much later in life. For instance, I became a teacher because I liked my uncle Jack, a school superintendent. He was such a nice guy that I thought teaching must be nice too! However, after many years of teaching, I still didn't feel the right fit. Yet, I asked myself, "what's wrong with me?" My idol was a colleague in the same grade in the same classroom in the same school for 22 years and just loved it. Me? I was bored by Christmas and felt no sense of accomplishment.

However, there was nothing wrong with me; I was simply in the wrong job! After much soul searching and reading self help books galore, I undertook a comprehensive assessment of everything I had done in my life. I broke down those tasks into skills. I grouped them and I named them. To my surprise, my key skills, my "passion" included the 3 key things I always managed to get into trouble for! For instance, all my report cards from kindergarten to grade twelve said, "Barbara talks too much"….MMMMmmm, today I get paid for it. My mother used to chide for bringing home and helping kids that were having personal/interpersonal problems! MMMMM, todayI get paid for it. And my boss, the Superintendent of Education told me he wouldn't hire me as a school principal because I was "always challenging the system, trying to change things, to fix things". He didn't need anyone like that! Mmmmm….today I get paid for it!

Barbara J. Bowes, FCHRP, CMC, CCP, M.Ed

OCTOBER 1

Affirmation: *"Forgive yourself for your faults and your mistakes and move on"*. —Les Brown

Justine was very remorseful because she spent most of her years incarcerated for a crime that she committed. Justine knew that she was wrong for committing the crime and she wondered how she was going to move ahead from this point. In order for Justine to move forward she knew that she must forgive herself for the mistakes that she had made.

Forgiveness brings a healing balm into your life. Forgiveness destroys the chains that have encompassed your life. Forgiveness frees you from all captivity, hurts, sorrow and pain. The pain from failure, relationships, abuse, addictions and fear are broken now. You are healed from being bruised and broken because your cycle has been changed and you are in a new season. This is your season of progression and momentum because forgiveness is priceless and it liberates you to move forward. Forgive yourself from your past faults and mistakes and move forward.

Donna Anderson

OCTOBER 2

"A word fitly spoken is like apples of gold in pictures of silver."
—Proverbs 25:11

Affirmation: *Embrace the power of well- spoken words.*

Oh, the necessity of speaking to others with well chosen words that dispel darkness and shed light. Oh, the need to first listen for understanding and speak less; cease from senseless babbling, and speak with the knowledge that we all have issues or concerns that may be unsettling. Compassion and empathy is required, not condemnation and criticism.

Oh, the need to speak in a spirit of love, to bridle the tongue and if nothing good can come forth, to be silent and wait for God to tell you what to say and when. At times, the period of "waiting" can seem like an eternity. Yet, trust that those quiet moments with God will deposits nuggets of wisdom in your soul and in due season the wisdom God has so graciously bestowed will be used in constructive and meaningful ways. Let your words be motivating, loving, and sincere; without contradiction or confusion.

Let your words ring with the steady assurance that God is the source for all good, sound, reasonable, and restored living. Speak words of peace, joy, love, hope, trust and forgiveness. Calm them that are down trodden and restore a right relationship with others as you daily walk with God. Yes, let the words you choose be as fine gold that shines brightly. May you encourage others and yourself to stay the course with the great navigator, our Lord and Savior, Jesus Christ.

Betty Patterson Shadrick

OCTOBER 3

"Today I trust my inner voice. I know my inner voice to be true and free from self-doubt"

At times, has it been easy for others to discourage you from following through with a great idea? Or have you discouraged yourself through negative self-talk and self-doubt?

Know that you do not have to keep going back to this place of self-doubt! You have a choice whether you want to keep self-doubt and negative self-talk in the driver seat.

It is all about energy and where you choose to put that energy. Yes – you do have that strength! You do have the inner power to shove those self-doubts on the backseat and leave them there for good!

How? It is a process. It may not happen overnight. But as soon as you engage in the process and you hold yourself accountable for following through – you will succeed! These self-doubts are made of nothing other than the energy of fear. If you allow this fear to dictate what directions in life you are taking then it becomes the dis-empowering energy that will feed you with all the unhealthy thoughts of self-doubt just to keep you from moving forward.

"You gain strength, courage and confidence by every experience in which you really stop to look fear in the face.
You are able to say to yourself, 'I have lived through this horror.
I can take the next thing that comes along.
You must do the thing you think you cannot do. "
—Eleanor Roosevelt

Gabriela Eikeland

OCTOBER 4

Affirmation: *I focus on what I want to create.*

Where you put your attention and what you focus on you create. Current scientific thinking – quantum physics, chaos theory and non-linear mathematics – validates that we function like magnets and radio transmitters. Although you might consider yourself to be a solid mass moving about through time and space, you are a field of energy vibrating at many different frequencies and sending out energetic messages on a continual basis. Every thought, feeling and action you express carries a vibration and that vibration attracts other like vibrations.

The Law of Attraction defines how energy fields of similar vibration are drawn, or magnetized together. Like attracts like. You are at all times attracting to you based on the vibrations that you are radiating and these vibrations are determined by where you are putting your attention.

The key is, are you attracting intentionally, or are you attracting by default? Attracting by default is the same as sending out a mixture of energy signals - some related to what you want, some related to what you don't want - then receiving back what seems like a random mix of desirable and undesirable results. However, nothing is random. Mixed focus creates mixed results.

Being intentional about the results you want to create aligns your energy to create them. When you are not consciously intending, you align your energy with whatever you focus on. When you focus on what you dislike in your life - being in debt, hating your job, bad things always seem to happen to you - you are actually attracting more of that. When you focus on what you want to create, you attract the opportunities, people and resources to make that your reality.

Janet Christensen

OCTOBER 5

Affirmation: *I will not be too proud, or too afraid to ask for help.*

Haiku   I asked friends to pray
And I am overwhelmed with love.
My thanks know no bounds.

Sometimes, we women find it difficult to ask for help. We're supposed to be able to do it all: work, raise a family, clean house, and "bring home the bacon". How did we get here? We don't ask for help. Women are the thread that weaves the fabric of society. Let's ask for help and create a beautiful tapestry together.

Dana D. Cable

OCTOBER 6

"I pray that the Lord richly blessed you
with everything you want out of life." —Helen Carr

Today is my grandmother's 90th birthday! Helen Carr is not someone you'll read about in a history book or hear about in the news. Despite this, she is an extraordinary person and has been one of my greatest life teachers. Too often we wait until a person passes away to show how important they are or wait till their eulogy to say that we love them. But I'm publically telling my grandmother today! We celebrate you today for all of the victories you've had in your life! And for all of the virtues you've passed along to me and your other five granddaughters.

The daughter of an Irish emigrant and African-American mother, she began her life in Chicago, Ill., and endured some hard early lessons as a bi-racial child growing up in the 1920s. Grandma Helen has thrived in the face of illness, suicide, abandonment, racism, alcoholism and death. Despite this, she has been a constant symbol of perseverance, faith, sacrifice, hard work, dedication, and love. My greatest lesson I've learned is the value and importance of family. Through it all, she has always put family above herself and everything else.

She has outlived her husband and the majority of her contemporaries; in fact less than 5 percent of the population lives to see age 90. But her long life has been purposeful. In her quiet, steadfast manner, Grandma Helen has taught me how to stay the course of life, no matter what obstacles are thrown in your way. She has stressed the value of independence and productivity in society. She has always encouraged me to make something of my life. And hopefully Grandma, you are well pleased.

Dawn Jamison

OCTOBER 7

"I was thought to be 'stuck up'. I wasn't. I was just sure of myself. This is and always has been an unfavorable quality to the unsure." —Bette Davis

Why is it that a woman is considered stuck up if she knows who she is, what she will or will not take, and doesn't mind saying so? Confidence and ego are not the same by any stretch of one's imagination.

I was introduced to my husband by a mutual friend. On one occasion when the friend was in town, I went to visit him. During my visit I happened to tell them about a vacation that I had taken to the Virgin Islands. At the time, I did not think anything of my attitude or behavior. However, I know that I can be quite animated when sharing a story. Nonetheless, to my surprise, I found out later, that my future husband thought that I acted "stuck up" because he thought that I was bragging when I described my adventures during my vacation. However, after he got to really know me better, he realized that I was a confident woman who loved to travel and have fun. Needless to say, we eventually had the opportunity to travel together to the Bahamas, Los Angeles, Las Vegas, and many other places. Throughout those times, I fondly remember how he enjoyed watching "me be me" as we made memories together.

Self esteem and ego are not synonymous although often confused.

Ann Ransom

OCTOBER 8

Affirmation: *I will be kind to Mother Earth and all the beautiful creatures.*

Haiku: We shared a moment,
Beautiful doe looked at me,
Peaceful communion.

We live in a techno world, connected by satellites and computers, disconnected from the ground we stand on and the many species who share our space. The greatest and the least has a place and I will honor all of creation.

Dana D. Cable

OCTOBER 9

"Remember…there is always a little girl in the stands that wants to be just like you…don't disappoint her." —Unknown

My mom has always been my hero. She took care of me. She played with me. She gave me space to grow and learn. She taught me the things I needed to know. She told me no and she didn't let me do what I wanted all the time. She was mean (I thought.)

But, now that I am a mom, I have realized that it's not that easy being a mom.

Kids don't come with an instruction manual. You can read all the latest books, take parenting classes to learn some skills, and do everything "just right," but you never really know for sure. Each day brings new and exciting questions for which I pretend to have an answer for. Sometimes I actually know the answer and other times, I don't know the answer…so I wing it.

I know that my children are watching me and idolizing me in the same way that I did my mom. Sometimes I am proud of my mothering and other times, not so much. I make mistakes. I may sometimes be too harsh or too overprotective. I may sometimes be too lenient and too permissive. But sometimes, I say the right thing and I do the right thing and hope that love will make up for all the rest.

I can only hope to take the lessons my mother taught me, add in a few pearls of my own wisdom, and pass the torch of motherhood one day to my daughters…who won't get it either…until they become mothers.

Dr. Joanne Siebert, D.C.

OCTOBER 10

"There is a growing strength in women but it's in the forehead, not the forearm." —Beverly Sills

You can accomplish anything with commitment and perseverance.
You should regularly remind yourself of the range of your accomplishments. You should give the same value to both small and large achievements. Whether small or large, any success is always preceded by commitment to the task and staying with it until it is done.

If you feel uninspired, take a moment to reflect on your past successes. You are reminded of your strength. Realize how powerful you are. You know that my strength can help you to do even greater things in the future.

All you need to do is to commit and persevere.

Whenever you come upon a challenge in a task, imagine your joy at the outcome and this should help you to commit and persevere until you achieve success once again. Remember you deserving of the greatness that lies ahead.

Words of empowerment:
Today, I believe that I can accomplish anything through commitment and perseverance. I see every obstacle as a chance to show what else is up my sleeve. I surprise myself with each attribute I display. I am driven to succeed because I know I can.

Judith Duclot-Fletcher

OCTOBER 11

Affirmation: *Keep your face to the sunshine and you cannot see a shadow.*

Live your life for today with hope in your heart and don't dwell on the past. Your past does not dictate your future.

Linda Ellis Eastman

OCTOBER 12

Affirmation: *"Life's obstacles will not become road blocks for my success."*

A few weeks ago, I stopped in to visit my dad on a Saturday morning and noticed that the yard had been freshly mowed. My sister was there so I asked who had mowed the lawn. She proudly announced that it was her. She then went on to tell me that it was the first time she had driven my dad's small tractor. So I naturally asked her how it went. She proceeded to tell me that she had a few minor mishaps. She ran into the side of the garage, knocked over several of the landscaping bricks, mowed over a small plant, put a dent in the fence, and came very close (but did not hit) my dad's car. As I was listening to her very vivid and animated description, I could easily visualize all of this occurring. We both laughed and made jokes about the experience.

This morning when I was talking with my sister over the phone, I asked how her handling of the tractor was going. I asked if she had mastered using it. Her response was "Yes. Now that I've removed all of the obstacles, I can do it quite well."

In most anything in we do in life, removing obstacles makes achieving success easier. In many cases, the most difficult part is identifying the obstacle. Once we can identify it, we can then take the necessary steps to remove it. What obstacles do you have in your way? What can you do to remove them?

Here is a good quote to remember this philosophy: *"You become limitless when you overcome what holds you back"* – Lorii Myers

Judy Singleton

OCTOBER 13

Affirmation: *"Forget the past."* —Nelson Mandela

Forget the past and focus on your future. The past should be used as a stepping stone to build upon your future. The past is a bridge between your present and your future. Cross the bridge, exceed and do great exploits. Your past no longer has control over your life because you decide your destiny. Learn from your past and bridge the gap between your past and your present. Guard your heart because it is time for you rise and go forward. The pain and failures of your past no longer hold you in captivity. Do not let your past experiences hold your captive because your future is bright. You can live a victorious life today as you make the decision to move forward. It is time to forget your past and embrace your future.

Donna Anderson

OCTOBER 14

"Success comes to a person who refuses to give up."
—Robert H. Schuler

Affirmation: *Today we affirm to never, ever, ever give up. We press forward, determined to reach and achieve our goals.*

Change is the one constant about life. As daylight gives way to midnight, as the seasons change, as your children grow up and join the ranks of adulthood, or parents age and require your assistance to negotiate their affairs and well-being; change is inherent in the ebb and flow of life's journey. Often, we welcome the exhilaration of new beginnings, the opening of new doors of opportunities. Then, we languish with feelings of uncertainty when doors once open are now closed. It may seem we have entered a dry season, a drought where things appear to have died and turned to dust.

Yet, the dry season has a purpose, it's designed to make us pause, re-assess our goals, ambitions, dreams and desires. The dry season forces us to look introspectively within and then challenges us to never, ever give up. During this season, we must be proactive and speak life to the situation. We say: "I can!" We adopt an attitude that perseveres, we believe we can succeed, and we actively pursue goals that will ultimately yield the "best fruits" of our labor. To yield the fruit of our labors, we make sure our goals have personal meaning; it involves an investment of our heart. We break our goals into measureable units-short term, mid-term, long term and life goals. We see ourselves achieving the goal. We affirm: "If we can conceive, we can achieve it! Today, we see ourselves as successful individuals, who can and will make a positive impact in our community and our world.

Betty Patterson Shadrick

OCTOBER 15

Affirmation: *It's now or never*

You know it's never too late to change? Push forward and keep learning new things everyday. Have something to look forward to. It could be now or never for someone who wants to quit drinking, smoking, get married, lose weight or go to college. You just never know. Be awake and in the moment. Now or never could happen at the most unexpected time in your life. Be spontaneous and go with your gut. You'll know when its time. Stay in the flow of life and ride the wave. This is your life and your race. Don't miss the opportunity to take a risk and try. If you don't take the risk you'll never know. Don't have regrets. Just do it NOW; no better time! Watch for the signs. If you are in the moment, aware and wanting answers you will find them. God has you in the palm of his hands. Create god karma in your life. What you give out you get back. If you don't take care of the issue the first time, believe me the problem will continue to come back over and over again until you take care of it. Deal with conflict. Stop pushing it under the rug. Show yourself how to take charge and be more in control of your life. Shoulders back, feet on the ground and say what you mean. Move on and keep becoming more whole. Practice being the best you can be. I challenge you to start TODAY. You never know whom you will inspire, or who's watching you. Be a blessing to someone. Find your strengths and passion and give back. After all isn't that what we're for? Step up to the plate. find your true calling. Show and give the world your creativity. Go for the gusto.

Angie Schultz

OCTOBER 16

Affirmation: *I choose to live in this moment, right now.*

Have you ever noticed how the consumer merchant scene drastically moves us so quickly ahead of ourselves. Argggghhhhh! In August, Halloween and Christmas show up. Puhleeze! Can I just enjoy August without the teasing witch laughing at me in Cracker Barrel? And, where are the apples and Neil Diamond singing 'September Morn' for September as the Christmas ornaments are choking my eyesight!?! Come on, now.

What if I just allow this day, October 16th, to be a simple moment in which to live?

What if I just assign this day with a precious beauty all its own?

What if I remember that little bible verse 'This is the day that the Lord has made'?

What if I choose to live in this moment right now?

I can do this!

Hello, sweet October 16th. Here I am to celebrate your day!

Lovin' it!

Sharon McWilliams

OCTOBER 17

"Tis the human touch in this world that counts,
the touch of your hand and mine." —Spencer Michael Free

Affirmation: *Today we extend a loving touch to others.*

Many of us express appreciation and love to those who have won a special place in our hearts and minds. Maintaining and sustaining relationships provides priceless moments to openly demonstrate the concern we have for our family and friends.

Yet, should our demonstrations of care and concern be restricted to only those holding places of endearment? Could we express tenderness to those we know less well, or even to a stranger? Farfetched as this notion may seem, it's not an unhealthy gesture to try.

A word of encouragement to someone in despair, a kind touch to someone bereft with care, a listening ear to another's story of woe, a friendly smile to someone whose face is wretched with the pain and frustration of life; are all loving touches which may brighten another's day, be healing salve to another's sorrows, and provide hope to the hopeless.

We are all part of this wonderful and yes, challenging existence called life. As we travel this journey, our passage may be richer, fuller, happier, and even saner, if we take the time to extend a loving touch to others along the way.

Betty Patterson Shadrick

OCTOBER 18

Affirmation: *"Our deepest fear is not that we are inadequate. Our deepest fear is that we are powerful beyond measure. It is our light, not our darkness that most frightens us. We ask ourselves, who am I to be brilliant, gorgeous, talented, fabulous?"* —Marianne Williamson

What if you were powerful beyond measure - brilliant, gorgeous, talented, and fabulous? It's a scary thought to confront - the idea that you might be powerful beyond measure. It makes all our actions and inactions carry so much weight. To think about what we could be doing to affect the world around us every day. If you felt powerful beyond measure, what would you do differently with your life? Is fear holding you back from feeling the power within you? If it is, feel it, and go out and do it anyways. YOU are powerful!

Marcie Wingfield Shanks

OCTOBER 19

"M" is for the million things she gave me,
"O" means only that she's growing old,
"T" is for the tears she shed to save me,"H" is for her heart of purest gold;
"E" is for her eyes, with love-light shining,
"R" means right, and right she'll always be,
Put them all together, they spell "MOTHER,"
A word that means the world to me.
—Howard Johnson

Affirmation: *Today we remember and pay tribute to our mother.*

She was a gifted, talented, loving, caring, diligent, and committed matriarch. Beautiful inside and out, our mother was both friend and confidant. You bore six children, three while only 20 years old. Then in the span of four to twenty years, three additional children were added to the family. You worked most of your life taking on various roles of responsibility: housekeeper, beautician, gourmet chef, and entrepreneur. In the process, you taught all your children to be kind, helpful to others, and supportive of each other. The importance of family was always emphasized and when one member was in trouble we were taught to rally with help and support.

Despite the trials and disappointments you endured, your innately kind demeanor remained unchanged. Thank you, Momma for teaching us lifelong lessons for living. Those lessons have sustained us all our lives. Thank you, Momma for encouraging your children's growth and development. Thank you, dear precious Momma, for being a listening ear when we needed to talk and for giving sound wisdom and instruction.

Thank you, dear Momma for the songs you lifted to Zion and the deliciously prepared meals. You brought beauty, peace, and relief to all you knew and loved. And, while you have made your earthly transition, we will see you again one day in Heaven.

Betty Patterson Shadrick

OCTOBER 20

Affirmation: *"I've learned that people will forget what you said, people will forget what you did, but people will never forget how you made them feel."*
—Maya Angelou

We all have people in our lives that genuinely care and make us feel valued and important. There are people that accept you as you are with unconditional love. These people make us feel significant and we savor our time spent with them. They leave a lasting impression and a delightful fragrance. We want to emulate them.

Think of a flower:

- A rose is beautiful but has prickly thorns
- A marigold is pretty unfortunately it stinks
- A daylily is beautiful but has no scent
- A heliotrope attracts bees, but some have allergic skin reactions; and
- A gardenia is beautiful with a delightful aroma

People that value you are like the beautiful and fragrant gardenia. We all cherish those people in our lives that listen and affirm us. All of us know of or have met roses, marigolds, daylilies and heliotropes; we may even be like those flowers!

We can spread love, kindness and acceptance to all those we meet and know by being like the beautiful gardenia with the delightful aroma.

Lori Tsugawa Whaley

OCTOBER 21

"Often, out of our greatest rejection comes our greatest direction."
—Joel Osteen

When rejection comes your way, it is difficult to see how any good can come from it or that there is a blessing in it. When a door closes, a relationship ends, a business folds or a job is lost, you may find yourself in a place of hopelessness and uncertainty about your future.

A reality about life is that rejection will occur. Your response to rejection determines your experience, whether positive or negative. You can take rejection and find a new direction or you can allow rejection to bring on depression and loneliness.

People may reject you and they will stop you in your tracks if you allow them. My niece lives life in such a way that she does not allow other people's negative opinions of her to hinder her from following her dreams and pursing her goals. Rejection fuels her determination to succeed.

If you are facing rejection today, I encourage you to rise above it by releasing other people's fears and limitations about you; thinking positively about your life and making the changes that will move you forward. Allow rejection to lead you to new direction and insight.

Be inspired knowing that the best is yet to come for you.

Affirmation: *I will rise above rejection.*

Frenetta Tate

OCTOBER 22

Affirmation: *Let go of the 'Issues in your Tissues' and instead hold onto the 'Healing Feeling!'* —Martha Moore Stevens

Are you holding pain, tension or disEASE anywhere in your body? The link between our physical bodies and emotions is strong. We often don't realize how much we hold onto in our physical bodies. Emotions such as anger or frustration get caught right in our neck, shoulder, stomach or back. Think of the phrase, "He's a pain in the __ neck? haha. The next time you feel ill or have pain/discomfort anywhere in your body, allow yourself to contemplate possible emotional triggers that might be connected. Sometimes just **naming** and **claiming** the possible emotion is enough to **tame** the pain and help it dissipate. This is how you let go of the issues in your tissues! Next focus on a healing feeling. Image yourself feeling perfectly with lots of energy and vitality. Imagine your neck feeling great with free mobility, ease of movement and complete range of motion. Hold onto the feeling of how it feels to be well, vibrant, strong and healthy. Imagine that it **is** so ....NOW!

Name it
Claim it
Tame it
Let go of the issues in your tissues and instead
Hold onto the Healing Feeling!
Be Well!

Kim Evans

OCTOBER 23

Affirmation: *"I think we need the feminine qualities of leadership, which include attention to aesthetics and the environment, nurturing, affection, intuition and the qualities that make people feel safe and cared for."*
—Deepak Chopra

(This letter is to my daughter, Zoe, who every day of her life has inspired me to be a better mom, leader and person.)

Dear Zoe,

From the time you were born, I knew you were special. You came into the world in calm observation. You spent the first year of your life taking it all in, observing and analyzing.

You've been full of life ever since your first birthday. Your intuition manifested itself at a very young age. When most children were learning how to walk, you were learning how to lead.

You have always had the gift of being your authentic self. You don't tolerate injustice and you require that we act with kindness and compassion toward each other. For that reminder, I thank you.

You won't let me out of the house with a hair out of place. You are my confidante, my companion and my role model.

Because of you, I have learned that my words and actions have consequences. I have also learned that my words and actions can comfort and heal. I am grateful that you have taught me this as it serves me well in all of my other relationships.

You are perfect in every way. You embody strength and compassion. Your attention to detail is non-paralleled. You are wise beyond your years. You, my daughter, are simply amazing and I am grateful to have you in my life. Stay true to yourself and when you do, you will rise to the top. I will be proudly looking on.

Love, Mom

Jill Johns

OCTOBER 24

How far you go in life depends on your being tender with the young, compassionate with the aged, sympathetic with the striving and tolerant of the weak and strong. Someday in your life you will have been all of these."
—George Washington Carver

Not one of us can predict the future or know how we will fair on any given day. Furthermore, we can't dictate who will or will not come to our aid should the need arise. However, it is my summation that if we go about our lives truly treating others as we would want to be treated that God's divine providence will produce that "ram in the bush" for our situations, our times of need, and our times of comfort.

I spent my last birthday having dinner with my only grandson for the first time. During our time together, I said to him, "You can't imagine how much I love you." And he responded, "Yes, I can imagine."

Love, compassion, sympathy and tolerance are fruits of the Spirit.

Ann Ransom

OCTOBER 25

"We must work assiduously to aspire to excellence."
—Dr. Martin Luther King, Jr.

Affirmation: *Today we commit to pursuing an attitude of excellence.*

When I was in high school eons ago, I had the good fortune of being taught by a masterful African American English teacher, Dr. Jeremiah Cameron. In the midst of exposing us to classic literature- Shakespeare, Emerson, Dickens, Hawthorne and others- he also liberally shared many of his favorite sayings. I've since realized they were actually instructions for living life with integrity and purpose. Those sayings still resonant with me today and inform my view of life and its possibilities. Let me share some of them with you. Dr. Cameron admonished and encouraged all of us that: "A man's reach should exceed his grasp or what's the heavens for?" "Tell the truth and shame the devil." " If the blind lead the blind, they will both fall in a ditch."

Our phenomenal teacher and sage mentored us with the adeptness of a master craftsman. He especially valued excellence and showed us powerfully in actions and deeds, why adopting this mantra was important to living a full and rich life. A commitment to excellence involves expecting the best, striving to become the best that you are capable of being; believing and acting that you can be the best by using and developing the skills and talents that where uniquely given to you. Excellence does not settle for mediocrity not content to do just enough to get by. Excellence looks for more, expects more, and challenges you to reach high, dream big and aspire to greatness. Our beloved teacher is no longer with us. Yet, the values he instilled in the hearts and minds of his protégés live on.

Betty Patterson Shadrick

OCTOBER 26

"Every experience is precious and valuable when we are able to gasp the lesson it offers, the opportunity it affords ." —Susan L. Taylor

Affirmation: *Today we remain open to life's possibilities and proclaim we are vibrantly alive and well.*

For those of us who have reached over three scores of living, learning, growing, and experiencing the ebbs and crescents of life, we come into this new season with sober awareness that we have fewer years ahead of us than behind us. How we use the remaining time we have left is all so very important to the very quality of service we give, the lives touched , and the lessons learned and transferred to others. So with renewed vigor let's affirm: "We are vibrantly alive and well." Because we are still among the living, still seen and not viewed, there is still much to embrace, experience, savor and enjoy.

We no longer have the luxury to waste this precious commodity - time. Within the 24 hours of each day, we can carve out time to read an uplifting piece of literature, listen to rejuvenating music, take in the absolute splendor of the rising sun, feast on the beauty of nature, give love and encouragement to others, laugh, play with our beloved pets, take a walk, enjoy a soothing bubble bath, smile more and frown less. When it all comes down to living a vibrant life, it's a choice. The choice is largely in our hands and depends on our attitudes and beliefs.

Today, choose to live vibrantly, walk in victory, overcome fear of the unknown, and bring all your cares and concerns to the all knowing Father, our Lord and Savior, Jesus Christ.

Betty Patterson Shadrick

OCTOBER 27

Affirmation: *"I don't suffer from insanity, I enjoy every second of it"*.
—Anonymous

Mental health, or the lack of it, is an epidemic across our globe. Never before have we had such levels of people who are diagnosed with depression, bipolar, or other such conditions. It can be a hard path back from somewhere dark and alone.

I have had a disease, diagnosed since I was 19, that causes me pain every day. I have travelled that dark path through the recesses of my brain. I used to say all the time that I "suffered" from incredible pain constantly. Now, I simply state that I have pain.

The shift in my consciousness to move from 'suffer' to 'have' is profound.

Suffering is a choice that I make every day about what is happening to me. I can choose to focus on my pain, my restrictions in movement, that I can't wear high-heel shoes, the judgment in other's faces as they look at "the cripple" and the issues that medication bring. I do have another option.

I can chose to be grateful I am not yet in a wheelchair - defying every doctors' prediction for the last 20 years, the fact that I have an amazing brain that keeps me curious about life and learning, that fact that I have a wonderful husband in my life who takes care of me in those moments when I can't hold a hair brush, let alone use it.

I now enjoy beating the doctors' predictions. I enjoy the companionship of friends who see past my deformities to my heart. I enjoy showing that someone with the label 'disabled' can live a fuller and richer life than anyone gives credit for. I can enjoy the power of walking when I am not supposed to be able to. I can enjoy that pain as something to fight and stand up against and refuse to bow to, showing me how strong and powerful I am to overcome such things.

I offer you this view and ask you to choose each and every day to have and not to suffer.

Becky Paroz

OCTOBER 28

Dear Sparkling Soul,
I gave you these Gifts so you would share them.
Please don't hide them. I shine through you.
—The Universe

I believe each person came to this Earth to live a unique sparkle that no one else but you can live. Sparkle is your divine essence – your signature on life. If you deny it, the world misses out. Allow it, and the world is made brighter.

Your job is to nurture that sparkle by sharing your gifts in big and small ways each day with all those willing to receive them. Some may partake, others may frown. This is not your concern.

Some people may not understand the gifts that flow through you. How could they? Those gifts are born to only you. You are the only one who has access to the wisdom in their birthing and creation.

So go forward. Make a joyful noise in celebration of what makes you uniquely YOU. Allow others their gifts as well. There is more than enough room in the garden of love for us all.

Paula Onysko

OCTOBER 29

Affirmation: *I am at peace in the present moment.*

"If you are depressed, you are living in the past. If you are anxious, you are living in the future.
If you are at peace, you are living in the present."
—Lao Tzu, ancient Chinese philosopher, founder of Taoism

Scientists estimate that the average person has between 60,000 and 80,000 thoughts a day, and that most of these thoughts are the same thoughts they were thinking the day before, the week before, the month before. For many people, the majority of these thoughts are negative and judgmental.

Lao Tzu's words speak eloquently to our thoughts and where they take us much of the time. We cannot change the past, and the future is unwritten. We only truly have the present moment. This is where peace is to be found.

Be aware of your thoughts. When you find yourself thinking negative things, stop yourself, and replace the negative focus by taking a deep breath and thinking of at least three things you are grateful for. This brings you back into the present moment, provides a positive focus and instills peace in your heart.

Janet Christensen

OCTOBER 30

Affirmation: *"Great minds discuss ideas; average minds discuss events; small minds discuss people."* —Eleanor Roosevelt

Great minds are big thinkers and great minds have the ability to change the world. It is exhilarating, stimulating and challenging to have a discussion about ideas. New ways of thinking are introduced and you gain insight and knowledge after a thought-provoking conversation. Your energy level soars.

Average minds discuss events and there are a myriad from which to choose. However, there are always two sides to every story. During discussions, disagreements can arise and the conversation can go ‹south›.

Small minds discuss people. I was taught to speak about a person as if they were present; that left less for me to talk about.

Eleanor Roosevelt was First Lady, writer and humanitarian who led a productive life. She stood against racial discrimination and was a spokesperson for the common person. Aside from being the longest-serving First Lady, Eleanor wrote six books. Criticized and loved, she set the bar high. Eleanor Roosevelt possessed a great mind. Eleanor Roosevelt changed the world. If we change our thoughts, we can change our world!

With a *(your?)* great mind engaged in discussing positive ideas, the possibilities are limitless!

Lori Tsugawa Whaley

OCTOBER 31

Affirmation: *The only thing worse than being blind, is having sight but no vision.* —Helen Keller

We are all gifted with the ability to have a vision. Close your eyes and think about what brings you a sense of purpose and passion. Lay out a plan to achieve this and let your vision become a reality.

Linda Ellis Eastman

NOVEMBER 1

"If you define abundance in terms of feeling there is plenty, you will be rich every day of your life." —Gurmukh and Cathryn Michon

There are too many places in our world where there is lack. You need only look at the headlines in your internet feed to see the countless children, women and men who are starving from lack of food. You only need to look at the television to see the many youth who have had a lack of education, and the homeless who have lack of shelter. These are the necessities of life that many people do not have and yet, many of us who have these basics and much more claim to be poor and in lack. Yet, I've heard many people, who grew up in large families and ate one meal a day say, "We didn't even know we were poor and hungry" because we had so much…" How is this possible?

Because we do not make the salary we are worth, live in the house we've always dreamt of, or drive the car we desire, we say that we are not rich. We might even say that life is unfair because we lack these things. If you are in this place, ask yourself the question, "What are you grateful for in your life?" Do you have a family, a friend, a shelter, a job, a piece of food, a book, God? Can you look at what you have and still feel rich? I challenge you today to claim your abundance, right now, by giving thanks for what you have.

Kymberley Clemons-Jones

NOVEMBER 2

Affirmation: *"I know that I am intelligent, because I know that I know nothing."* —Socrates

One of the great philosophers of all time. Socrates is known for many sayings, but this one is his most profound. He never wrote a line of text, but almost everyone still knows his name today.

He knew that we cannot know all things under the sun. In fact, some of the most dangerous people are those who are certain that they have all the answers for everybody else. Hitler comes to mind as an example of the dangers of absolutely certainty.

When I look for a coach or a mentor, I seek the one who annoys me the most. The one who says something that challenges me, makes me angry, or completely disagrees with me. Why? Because they will challenge my certainty, my knowledge, my assurance that I am right. And I want that, because I know, that ultimately, I know nothing.

Everything is a possibility. Allow others to demonstrate knowledge to you and be amazed and wondrous at all there is to learn. And then forget it and learn something else. It is in this way that we grow and develop, challenge the expectations of society.

So give yourself permission to believe you know nothing, and be assured that you have all the rest of the days of your life to seek more and more knowledge.

Becky Paroz

NOVEMBER 3

Affirmation: *All the world is full of suffering. It is also full of overcoming.*
—Helen Keller

Think about the challenges of your lifetime and the many times you have overcome these obstacles. The next time you feel you just can't go on, remember the times when you have gained the strength to overcome those past difficulties. Reach deep within and know you can face whatever comes along, head-on!

Linda Ellis Eastman

NOVEMBER 4

"Voting is the most precious right of every citizen, and we have a moral obligation to ensure the integrity of our voting process." — Hillary Clinton

Today is Election Day in the U.S.! It's our opportunity to cast a vote for the candidates we feel best represent our interests and voices. The day when we let our voices be heard on proposed legislation in our respective cities, states and country. According to media reports, 2012 voter turnout was only 57.5 percent. This was the lowest turnout rate since the 2000 election. This statistic tells us that nearly half of Americans choose to stay home or perhaps, experienced voting barriers.

My biggest fear is that people just don't care enough to vote. In the past century, countless people have given their lives for the opportunity for women and minorities to cast their ballots and let their voices be heard. I urge voters, not to take this task lightly.

If you feel disenfranchised or aren't happy with the candidates on the ballot, vote. Every vote must be counted and makes a difference. Here are five easy things you can do to get involved: 1. Register to vote, 2. encourage someone else to register, 3. do your homework on the pressing issues and prospective candidates, 4. watch or attend candidate debates, or 5. volunteer to work at the voting polls.

At the very least, be a good civic role model for your children or young people in your community! Stress the value of the democratic process and lead by example!

Dawn Jamison

NOVEMBER 5

"Thanksgiving prompts the spirit of humility. Genuine gratitude to God for His mercy, His abundance, His protection, His smile of favor."
—Charles R. Swindoll

Affirmation: *This month we are thankful for our many blessings.*

Being truly thankful is an art that develops with time and with living. As children we were often admonished by our parents to say thank you for courtesies and gifts bestowed by others and to give thanks for the food prepared to nourish our growing and developing bodies.

As youngsters, we accepted our parental upbringing with little question. The values taught and instilled were tacitly understood as the right thing to do. Many times our thank you's were little more than perfunctory social courtesies; nonetheless, they were said.

Now, as adults, we need to remember and reclaim some of the earlier innocence we had as children and transform it into the art of being thankful for all that enters our lives. The triumphs, the disappointments, the laughs, the tears, and ups as well as the downs, are part of our repertoire of life. Through it all we must always remember that having a thankful spirit will help us move gracefully through the sun and storms of life.

As we enter the Thanksgiving season, let's strive to remain thankful for life, thankful for the opportunity to grow and maximize our potential and thankful for being part of humanity.

Betty Patterson Shadrick

NOVEMBER 6

Affirmation: *You must do those things you think you cannot do.*
—Eleanor Roosevelt

Face your fears. Try something you have always wanted to do but were afraid to try.

Have no regrets about life. Live life to the fullest and don't be held back by your fears.

Linda Ellis Eastman

NOVEMBER 7

Affirmation: *"I am willing to forgive others who have wronged me."*

Typically during the month of November we promote being thankful, but in order to be truly thankful we need to be forgiving as well. As children, we look to adults to learn and grow—when in reality, adults can learn from children. Ever noticed that when children have disagreements with each other they don't stay mad for very long? This is because they easily forgive one another and move on.

Forgiveness is not saying that what the person did was okay. It is simply saying that we have accepted what happened and we are choosing to forgive so that we can progress. We are taking control of the situation rather than letting the actions and/or words of others control our thoughts or feelings. Forgiveness does not mean forgetting what happened, it means that we have learned from the situation and we are going to use that as a tool for the future.

We can all learn the art of forgiveness and will be amazed at the sense of freedom we gain when we are able to forgive. Lewis B. Smedes has said *"To forgive is to set a prisoner free and discover the prisoner was you."* Who can you forgive today?

Judy Singleton

NOVEMBER 8

The kingdom of heaven is like a grain of mustard seed that a man took and sowed in his field. It is the smallest of all seeds, but when it has grown it is larger than all the garden plants and becomes a tree, so that the birds of the air come and make nests in its branches. —Matthew 13:31-32

When I wake in the morning the first thing I do is take stock of who I am, who I am being asked to be or something I am being asked to do each day. I sort through the chaff and find the wheat or coal and find the diamond. Once I find the Wheat / Diamond that is ME, I know my emotional bank is filled up for the day.

I remember who I am at the heart of me - a woman, a daughter, a sister, a friend and an aunt; I breathe. Once I remind myself of who my family and friends knows me to be, an honest, hardworking, truthful woman, I take another breath. And last I remind myself of who my GOD knows me to be the woman he created with integrity, loyalty, honesty, honor and grace for days. Breathing easier and normal by the third breath of my morning, I face the day with Faith that I am right with me.

I am okay with who I am, the decisions I have made throughout my life both good and not so good. Lastly, I have to accept what my character represents. Some days my character is shinier, less tarnished than others but for the most part I am at peace each day. This is the faith I have in me.

Once I take stock at the beginning of each day, I am deeply relieved at who and what I am. This is the Faith I have in me; this is the faith I have in others. This comes from my Father, Boyce L. McLeskey. Faith starts out small then grows by leaps and bounds each day!

Michele McLeskey

NOVEMBER 9

Affirmation: *I will Dream Big and Go For It!*

Haiku: Writing time has come,
A journey long foreseen and
Now becoming real.

No dream is too small or too big. Pursue them. If you want to be in relationship – explore all possibilities. If you want to write, paint, sing, dance – explore all possibilities. If you want to run, swim, bike – explore all possibilities. Jump out of a plane, fly across the ocean, climb a mountain, travel the world – explore all possibilities.

The answer to living the dream might be just around the corner.

Dana D. Cable

NOVEMBER 10

Affirmation: *I am empowered.*

What does being empowered require?

You take full responsibility for your actions and your results.

You are aware that you are always making choices and fully accept that where you are today is a direct result of the choices you have made.

You refuse to be a victim or to blame others for your circumstances.

You understand that if you want to change where you are in the future, you will need to make different choices to create these different results.

You have integrity and respect for yourself and others.

You are an authentic leader.

What does being empowered look like?

Inspiring! Confident! Courageous! Passionate! Curious! Creative! Trustworthy! Amazing! Fabulous!...

Janet Christensen

NOVEMBER 11

Affirmation: *"I acknowledge and appreciate the contributions of others to my life."*

The impact and contributions that other people make to your life and the quality of your experience of it are tremendous. Perhaps it is in the form of sacrifice, such as your parents giving things up so you could have more, soldiers giving their lives and/or fighting for freedom, or a friend dropping everything when you need them. It might be in the form of a gift; of time, attention, appreciation, a compliment, a present, or something else. It might also be through adversity; a struggle that helped you become stronger, a difficult relationship that you learned from, a loss that you survived. All of these situations represent contributions that were made, either directly or indirectly, to your life.

Make a point of acknowledging and appreciating the contributions that others have made and continue to make to your life, both to yourself and to them.

Michelle Richardson

NOVEMBER 12

"It's hard to fight an enemy who has outposts in your head."
—Sally Kempton

Each morning the sun rises is an opportunity to reaffirm your morals.
You are prepared for every day you are blessed with. You see the rising sun as an opportunity to reaffirm your morals. Allow your morals to take you through the roughest situations each day and emerge unscathed.

Your morals are challenged each day by negative people and situations. When you reaffirm your morals each morning, you are newly equipped with the tools to handle any negative situation. You are able to take the high road when you recommit to your morals and beliefs each day.

If you encounter situations when you are forced to choose a course of action, choose based on your beliefs. Choose to remain upright than to compromise your beliefs.

Affirmation: *Today, I commit to preventing other desires from forcing me to compromise my beliefs. I believe my path is leading me toward success.*

Judith Duclot-Fletcher

NOVEMBER 13

May the Warm Winds of Heaven
Slow softly upon your house.
May the Great Spirit
Bless all who enter there.
May your Moccasins
Make happy tracks
In many snows,
And may the Rainbow
Always touch your shoulder.
—Cherokee Prayer Blessing

Thanksgiving is just around the corner. We plan what to cook, drink, the folks we'll talk to, and prepare for our day off. We feel blessed to have food on our table and a roof over our head. But make sure to give thanks for all the blessings, no matter how small. Think about what you can do to bless others through thoughts and actions. Practice a random act of kindness within your community. Pay for someone else's coffee. Take tea to someone having a rough day. Give a blanket to a homeless shelter. Pick up groceries for an elderly shut-in. Pay for a veterans coffee. Discard extra coats, shoes, blankets, sheets, towels, wash clothes, toiletries, and other clothing items at the Salvation Army for distribution to those in need. Help out a Soup Kitchen. And, talk about starting a Charity Dinner club.

Charity dinner clubs started with the **The Third Thursday Charity Dinner Club**. It grew out of a group of former Readers Digest co-workers who met for dinner on the third Thursday of the month to catch up. Instead of talking about others and gossiping, they discussed charities that needed a little help through time and donations. Each member took on a volunteer project. At dinner, they updated the others on the current and upcoming projects, brainstormed new ideas and shared personal stories of success through their efforts.

This Thanksgiving, invite friends, family, loved ones, or special coworkers who are willing to commit 90 minutes a month to talk about helping community charities.

Katrina Everhart

NOVEMBER 14

Affirmation: *To fail is human; to rise again from the ashes is a gift.*

Think of the many times you have fallen or failed. You have risen time and time again. Take a moment now to reflect upon the gifts you have been given. Continue to have faith that when you fall again, you have the strength to rise once again.

Linda Ellis Eastman

NOVEMBER 15

Affirmation: *Change your "Stinking Thinking" because your brain believes everything you say!*

Our thoughts originate in our frontal cortex which is connected to a part of the brain called the hypothalamus. The hypothalamus houses the pituitary gland which is the master gland controlling many neurotransmitters, hormones and endocrine function. Literally our thoughts trigger a biochemical event. This becomes very important when we realize that our brains believe everything we say. How many of us have said, "Oh, I'll never lose this weight", "I'll never get out of debt" or "I hate this job?" These thoughts that we think in our conscious brain reflect only 10 % of our thinking. These are then magnified by the other 90%, our subconscious thinking. When we continue disempowering thoughts, all of our body chemistry works toward this end. On average we have 60,000 thoughts per day and 75% of these are commonly negative. How about if we consciously choose to replace our "stinking thinking" with more positive thoughts? How about telling ourselves, "Thank God, I'm rich!", "I am my ideal weight" or "I have infinite abundance in my life", "I am loved and honored in all ways" or "I am grateful for all that I have and all of my life experiences?" Observe how the body/mind works to create these affirmations and/ or responds differently to challenging situations. You have nothing to lose and everything to gain! So start today replacing your "stinking thinking" with positive, affirming, happy thoughts. You will be amazed at how much better you feel! You may also be quite pleased as some of the positive thoughts manifest into life goals and dreams.

Kim Evans

NOVEMBER 16

Affirmation: *I will listen to the wisdom of older women.*

Haiku: My heart is well-served
In the company of Wise
Wonderful Women.

In today's world "crone" has a negative connotation. But our early ancestors honored the "Crones" – the elder, wise women of the village. If there are "crones" in your village, seek them out. You might be surprised at the wit, the wisdom, and the joy of living that is shared by these women. You too, will one day be a "crone".

Dana D. Cable

NOVEMBER 17

A dream doesn't become reality through magic; it takes sweat, determination and hard work. —Colin Powell

Anything is possible if you believe it and act on it by putting your belief in action. This world is vast. There is a supply for every demand. Whatever idea or dream you have is not a trifle or impossibility. Many have done outstanding things that were once deemed impossible.

Fred Smith, Founder of Federal Express wrote a term paper based on an idea for reliable overnight delivery. His professor gave him a C because the idea "wasn't feasible." Fred believed in his idea. Today, Federal Express is a very profitable company. When naysayers say "no" to your great idea or dream; they are just not the ones to help you bring it to fruition.

You must keep believing in your dream and putting action behind that belief. Don't let the fact that others do not understand your idea or dream to cause you to doubt yourself. If anything, let it fuel your willpower to keep pursuing your heart's desire.

Be inspired to make your dreams a reality with focus and determination.

Affirmation: *1 will put my beliefs into action.*

Frenetta Tate

NOVEMBER 18

Love is a better teacher than duty. —Albert Einstein

Lord, grant that I might not so much seek to be loved as to love.
—Francis of Assisi

As a child, I was blessed to have an older sister that loved little kids. She was like a second Mother to me. When our mother, of 6 kids, was not available to me I went to Connie Sue Kelsey Mouton Anderson. She is one of my best friends even now.

She taught me the meaning of Love for EVERYONE, no matter whom/what they were. She is so very kind of heart she accepts anyone for whatever reason. Her thoughts love in all forms. And her words are softly spoken and lovingly meant. She truly is the epitome of a genteel, gently breed, Southern Woman.

She teaches me what I want to emulate on my good days and what I should aspire to be on my bad ones. So daily, I have a wonderful example of Love. If I didn't, I think I would still recognize this trait in others and seek out these people in which to resonate. For the example of Love from my sister Connie, I am eternally grateful for her strength of character in sharing this with me.

Michele McLeskey

NOVEMBER 19

Affirmation: *I stand in my personal power*

Everyone has occasions where they are confronted with difficult situations. How you respond in these situations can leave you feeling either positive and empowered, or regretful and victimized. The difference in outcome will depend of whether you stand in your power and choose your response, or if you get caught in the emotion of the situation, get your buttons pushed and react.

People commonly react to situations and issues in 4 ways by choosing to:

- Fight – the best defence is offence
- Flight – removing themselves from the situation instead of facing it
- Freeze – shutting down and not communicating
- Facade – pretending everything is okay. "I'm fine. Nothing is the matter."

Instead of reacting, you can choose to respond, stand in your personal power and create win/win situations.

Instead of fighting, choose to respond with **courtesy**.

Instead of taking flight, have **integrity** and face the issue.

Instead of freezing, choose to be **open** and communicate.

Instead of putting on a facade, be **honest** about your thoughts and feelings.

All four aspects – courtesy, integrity, openness and honesty – must be present. When you choose to respond this way, you are empowered and able to overcome your fears and insecurity. If the person does not like what you have to say, the world will not end. It is better to speak your truth than to sell yourself out. Commit to speak your truth on your terms, with courtesy, integrity, openness and honesty.

Janet Christensen

NOVEMBER 20

Affirmation: *"Somebody saw something in you once-and that is why you're where you are today. Thank them!"* —Don Ward

There have been people in your lives that have supported and believed in you. When you could not see your potential or believe in yourself, they were there encouraging you and being your ‹cheerleader›. You may have had a period in your life when it seemed impossible to change your situation. At the time that you needed it the most, your faithful parent, friend or 'angel' came along side of you and gave you exactly what you needed.

We all have different ways of showing appreciation. Here are a few ways you could thank that special person in your life:

- Write a thank you note
- Make a telephone call
- Bake a plate of cookies
- Handcraft a special item
- Send flowers or a gift card
- Prepare a meal and invite them; and/or
- Pay a special visit

A thoughtful gesture of appreciation will bring warmth and happiness. Don›t wait until they›re gone to share what is in your heart. Express your gratitude with a gesture meaningful to them.

During the month of November, our hearts are open when we think of Thanksgiving and our many blessings. This is an excellent time to remember the people in our lives that believed in us, gave us hope and made a difference in our world.

Lori Tsugawa Whaley

NOVEMBER 21

Affirmation: *"I am willing to let go of the things I cannot control."*

This affirmation is a difficult one for me. I like to be able to control most all situations because it makes me feel more confident about myself and relaxed in situations. If I am in control, then I know what to anticipate. Unfortunately, I cannot control all things in my life and those that I cannot, I need to learn to let go.

What I can control are my actions and emotions. This has been a lesson that has taken years for me to learn. Sometimes not being in control requires me to step out of my comfort zone. But, I have found that is okay. When I am stepping out of my comfort zone, I am typically learning or experiencing something new.

I have to have faith in God and those around me that things will work out when I do not have control. I must also look at what I can gain from the experience and how it can help me in the future. There are going to be a lot of situations I cannot control, but by relieving myself of the stress of thinking I could or should do something about it I am able to relax and learn from the experience.

This quote is a helpful reminder regarding this affirmation: *"Incredible change happens in your life when you decide to take control of what you do have power over instead of craving control over what you don't."*—Steve Maraboli.

Judy Singleton

NOVEMBER 22

I am God's abundant child, grateful and thankful for my many blessings.

Have you ever noticed how Thanksgiving is overlooked in the consumer merchant scene, crowded out by Halloween and Christmas?

What happened that we hurry through a beautiful holiday, holy day, where we can be so grateful for our abundance of blessings?

Have we forgotten to count them and to be thankful? Have we gotten caught up in the buying and the early morning sales with all the rush to the doors and the grabbing as if there is no tomorrow?

What have we done to ourselves? What have we lost? Where is the honor and integrity of our thankfulness?

Do we get caught up in the 'not enough', and getting the 'right' gift at the 'right' price?

Are we in the snare of scarcity thinking?

Have we forgotten the abundance of God's gifts?

What if we choose each day in November to journal our gratitude, write it down, and say it out loud as we arise and before bedtime? We can sweetly roll right into Thanksgiving Day with such a grateful heart.

What if we focus on the simple pleasures and treasures of our lives, those things that don't carry a pricetag?

Is that price too great?

I think not.

Sharon McWilliams

NOVEMBER 23

Affirmation: *"My future is an unscripted movie—limitless"*

My son is an avid movie fan and he loves going to the cinema. Our family goes on a regular basis, but we always have to get there early so that we don't miss any of the coming attractions. To him, the previews are almost as important as the movie itself.

Albert Einstein once said, *"Imagination is everything. It is the preview of life's coming attractions."* This is such a great analogy. When we look at our lives, do we use our imagination to envision a future we want to see? Or are we so caught up in the immediate bustle of everyday life that we don't have time to use our imagination?

Think about the film clips shown for previews—they are purposely selected so that we will be intrigued and will want to know more about the movie and the characters. Do the thoughts of our future have us wanting to know more? Are we captivated by the endless possibilities of what we can do and/or accomplish? If not, now is the time to begin using the one thing that we were so good at using as children—imagination.

As adults, we often consider imagination an adolescent term—one that is not connected to adulthood. However, we all need to be able to create our future by utilizing our imagination. Without an imagination, we cannot dream and without dreams, we have nothing to believe in. Once we are able to imagine our dreams, we can begin to believe in ourselves and our abilities. As a result, we will reach our goals and in the end play out the scenes for our future lives.

Judy Singleton

NOVEMBER 24

Affirmation: *When diet is wrong, medicine is of no use.*
When diet is correct, medicine is of no need.
Ancient Ayruvedic Proverb

This Proverb still rings true today! Yet there is much confusion about what diet is correct. It seems that at any given time one of the 3 macronutrients - fats, carbohydrates or protein are ostracized. The truth of the matter is that **all** three macronutrients are critically important for proper metabolic function of your body. Yet there is a wide range of healthy versus unhealthy options within each macronutrient. Make it simple for yourself. Avoid fast food restaurants and highly processed foods. Choose instead items that are closer to how God created them.

Carbohydrates - Let most of your carbohydrates be fruits, vegetables, beans or low glycemic/high fiber whole grains. Avoid anything with or having derivatives of high fructose corn syrup.

Fats - Choose monounsaturated or polyunsaturated fats instead of saturated or transfats. Avoid anything that includes hydrogenated or partially hydrogenated oils. Instead eat avocados, walnuts, almonds, healthy nut butter, olives, or olive oil.

Protein - Choose plant based protein for most of your meals such as lentils, quinoa, or beans. If you do eat animal protein, make sure it's meat from animals that are grass fed without hormones or antibiotics.

If you want to explore a diet more precisely for your genetics, check out the APO E gene diet. This diet, based on science, is customized based on your own genetics and has been shown to prevent and even reverse inflammatory diseases such as heart disease and Alzheimer's disease. You can find out more at www.perfectgenediet.com.

Just for today, choose all healthy food!

Kim Evans

NOVEMBER 25

Affirmation: *"Think like a queen. A queen is not afraid to fail. Failure is another steppingstone to greatness."* —Oprah Winfrey

In June of 2013, leanin.org launched their "What would you do if you weren't afraid?" campaign. Women of all ages, backgrounds and experiences weigh in on tumblr and the responses have been intriguing and surprising.

The universal truth in this campaign is that we are all afraid and the fears range from changing hair styles to running for president.----

How can we inspire the next generation of women to release their fear?

I'll start by showing them the way.

I was afraid to blog and to write. To me, writing is a very permanent and concrete form of expression. Publishing written content opens me, my thoughts and my ideas up to criticism and misinterpretation. I am afraid that people will misinterpret my intentions. I don't want to be misinterpreted. It feels unsafe, uncomfortable and scary. But I'm doing it anyway.

I have learned to face my fear of failure. I have written things that people don't like and they've let me know they don't like it. And I'm still here. I'm still writing. Why? Because I enjoy it and it stretches me to reach outside my comfort zone. I'm still writing because I can choose to focus on the people who don't like what I have to say or on the people who DO like what I have to say. I choose the latter.

My message won't reach everyone and won't inspire all people in the same why. It inspires me and if I can positively inspire at least one other person in the world, I will have done my job.

So I ask you, what would you do if you weren't afraid?

Jill Johns

NOVEMBER 26

Affirmation: *Today I take time to be still, replenish my inner well and remember who I am.*

"Be still, loved one. God speaks in the silent spaces."

Take time today to be still and embrace the silence – the gaps of emptiness that require no filling. These are sacred moments to plug back in and remember: I am not my work. I am not my thoughts or my present circumstances. I am the voice, hands, heart, eyes and mind of the Divine. In me, is everything I need to thrive.

In stillness, allow your breath to deepen. Feel a warm glow in the centre of your heart, emanating outward in all directions. Feel your heartbeat pulsating throughout your body. Notice your thoughts. Notice the space between your thoughts. Allow your body to soften and become one with the world around you. You are not alone. You are whole, complete and connected to all living beings.

Keep your inner well full with this knowing. Return to this well whenever you have forgotten. Today nurture your body with sacred sleep, alive food and energizing movement that feels luxurious. As your well overflows, gift that to the world.

Paula Onysko

NOVEMBER 27

Celebrate your relationships.

In high school, our drama department put on the 1937 play, *You Can't Take it With You*, written by George S Kaufman and Moss Hart. At that time I didn't really think outside my own little world. And I had never truly contemplated the value of people and relationships in our lives. As I thought about this phrase, "you can't take it with you"; I started to realize that there is only one thing we can take with us: our relationships with others.

When my husband Chuck suddenly passed away at age 43, I immediately thought about the incredible blessing that he was taking with him, which is the relationships he created while here on Earth. I pictured his mother welcoming him into Heaven, and his uncles whom he loved dearly, and a baby brother who died as an infant who rejoiced in my husband's return. Then I pictured the eventual day when I die, that it will be a celebration of the relationships I've created here that will reunite together once again.

Those who go before us will be there to welcome us when our earthly life ends. I tell my young daughters how death is really a new beginning, full of hope and peace. And they need not fear the end of their lives, nor mine, nor any of their loved ones. Because when we cultivate good relationships here, we CAN take them with us! That is what I believe. It fills my heart. And it motivates me to live my best life now, while I still have the opportunity to impact the lives of others here, now, today.

Rebecca Sheperd

NOVEMBER 28

Affirmation: *Joy comes from putting another's welfare ahead of our own.*

Matthew 23-11: *The Greatest among you must become servant of all.* It brought great joy to Jesus to heal the sick, feed the hungry and preach the gospel to the poor.

John 12-26: *If any man serves me, let him follow me; and where I am there shall also my servant be; If any man serve me, him will my father honor.*

Cassandra Gaines

NOVEMBER 29

Affirmation: *"Do one thing everyday that scares you."* —Eleanor Roosevelt

We become comfortable in our routine and often go through the motions of our life without conscious awareness. Have you ever driven home from work and do not remember the drive?

Excitement is often coupled with anxiety and it can take us out of our comfort zone but it can also make us feel alive. We might feel uncomfortable when we try something new but the adrenaline throughout our body makes us a feeling of rush. It means we are growing and taking advantage of the opportunities of life. We are taking control of our life, rather than reacting to it.

Take Eleanor Roosevelt's advice today and do one thing that scares you just a little bit.

Maritza Rodriguez-Arseneau

NOVEMBER 30

"At least once a day, allow yourself the freedom to think and dream for yourself." —Albert Einstein

Children are naturally inquisitive and children have big dreams. Children see themselves as invincible and able to ‹conquer the world›. We can learn from the innocent and irrepressible ways children live their lives. Children are creative, imaginative, spontaneous, ingenious, artistic, innovative and most of all loveable! The young people of today will become the leaders of tomorrow.

Albert Einstein regarded his achievements as a step towards his next advancement. He won the 1921 Nobel Prize in Physics and is most known for $e=mc2$. Einstein spent time in solitude thinking. The practical applications of his discoveries include the development of:

- Television
- Remote devices
- Lasers; and
- DVD players.

Einstein had a profound influence on humanity today. His life touches all of our lives and our world is better because of his work. It is not a ‹luxury› to spend time to think and dream daily; it is vitally important. Einstein understood and practiced this discipline and freedom. Create a space and time to think.

Spend time to think and dream daily, like Einstein, and you may just unlock the next great leap forward for humanity!

Lori Tsugawa Whaley

DECEMBER 1

"Don't hold onto dead things."
—Holy Spirit's word to Author

There was a time, five years ago, that the Holy Spirit spoke to me saying, "Do not hold onto dead things." I didn't quite understand what the Holy Spirit meant by this although it was a time of great change in my life. I was moving into my first pastorate, going to a place drastically different than most to which I was accustomed. I was feeling an even more powerful pull to the Lord to do God's will no matter what anyone else thought. I knew life was changing and I assume that the Holy Spirit was making sure that as I moved in obedience that I would not try to hold onto those things from the past that would stop me from being obedient.

What were those dead things in my life? They were anything contrary to what the Creator was telling me to do. Like many of us, as the Creator was leading and guiding me in a certain direction there was a desire to sometimes hold onto things of the past, those things that would have taken me off the path that I was on and away from God's will for my life.

If I had listened to many of those around me, I would have been too afraid to take the step to walk into my season as a pastor. I would have talked myself out of coming to such a different place, a different denomination with different people, a different ethos if you will. I encourage those who read this today that it is okay to leave those dead things in your life behind and move into what God has for you.

Kymberley Clemons-Jones

DECEMBER 2

Affirmation: *Go the Extra Smile! :)* —Dr. Clifford Kuhn

This quote comes from my colleague, Dr. Clifford Kuhn, who is known nationally as the "Laff Dr." His infectious love of humor and positive emotions have greatly enriched my life. When I feel discouraged, frustrated or blue, I quickly think of "going the extra smile." It's amazing how just smiling - even if you think you have nothing to smile about, will raise your spirits and help you feel lighter. One of his favorite humor exercises is to have you put a big grin on your face, "like you're eating a banana sideways" grin, then turn and look at others with that grin. Pretty soon everyone around you is also grinning and everyone is feeling more light-hearted and happy. As Dr. Kuhn says, smiling will help you open up your "humor nature." There are many physical, psychological and emotional benefits to humor. Here are some of them. Humor can:

- Reduce stress
- Boosts the Immune system
- Relieve Pain
- Decrease Anxiety
- Stabilize your mood
- Enhance Communication
- Inspire Creativity
- Maintain hope
- Boost your Morale.

So the next time you feel down, put a smile on your face and "Go the Extra Smile." Your body, mind and Spirit will thank you for it! :)

Kim Evans

DECEMBER 3

"Today I have the courage to speak my truth"

How we communicate in the world often mirrors how we feel about ourselves.

Our tone of voice may reflect shyness and a fear of speaking up as we try to put our emotions and feelings into words.

Perhaps a dominating tone of voice, with the tendency to interrupt, is the result of negative past experiences where we have felt overpowered.

Whatever applies to you, remember that you are the main decision maker in your life and that the only expert on you is you.

You have the right to feel emotionally safe and you do not need to earn the right to speak your truth or to be heard.

Exercise your ability to communicate your feelings, ideas, and thoughts clearly and without fear.

Gabriela Eikeland

DECEMBER 4

*"Men are taught to apologize for their weaknesses,
women for their strengths."* —Lois Wyse

Letting others have the last word.
When it comes to having the last word, maybe you are happy to skip your turn. You are usually better off when you let others have the final say.

Your relationships run more smoothly when you stop struggling to win minor arguments. Caring about your friends and family matters more than proving that you are right.

Considering other people's points of view also helps to make your thinking more flexible. You become open to new perspectives and consider experimenting with fresh approaches.

As you practice listening to others, your respect for those around you grows. You feel like I understand them better when you listen and realize how much they can teach you. Your connections with them deepen as well.

Actions often matter more than words. Devote your time to activities that bring you closer to achieving your goals. This is a better use of your energy than getting caught up in discussions that may have little potential to yield tangible results.

Affirmation: *Today, I manage my emotions and hold my tongue when
I believe that this is the most constructive approach.* ***I am happy to let
others enjoy the satisfaction of having the last word.*** *I want us all to be
happy and fulfilled.*

Judith Duclot-Fletcher

DECEMBER 5

"The greatest good you can do for another is not just to share your riches, but reveal to him his own." —Benjamin Disraeli

There are many things I love about Christmas and one of my favorites is the "Angel Tree" in my community. My family and I are blessed to be able to choose several tags from the tree and provide gifts to children in need. My children choose the tag of a child near their own age and help shop for toys that this child might enjoy. Each year they have a deeper understanding of why we shop for "Angel Tree" gifts. My hope is that they are learning about compassion and service to others.

While I feel good about "sharing my riches," I have often wondered if this is the highest and best use of my "riches." Would it not be better to address the root cause of the need? Perhaps addressing unemployment, addiction or chronic poverty would serve the greater good. Perhaps breaking the cycle of abuse or building self-esteem is the answer.

I do not know the answer to this question.

So, I choose both.

I choose to brighten up a child's Christmas morning with gifts that their parents were not able to provide for whatever reason. I choose to think in some small way this shields a child from some of the reality of their situation.

I choose to support organizations in my community with both my time and my money in hopes that system-wide change will be a new reality. I choose to be the change I wish to see and I encourage you to do the same.

Many Blessings!

Dr. Joanne Siebert, D.C.

DECEMBER 6

Affirmation: *"I consider that a man's brain originally is like a little empty attic, and you have to stock it with such furniture as you choose".*
—Arthur Conan Doyle

Everyone has an ideal comfort zone, a look-and-feel that they particularly love, whether it be Mediterranean styling, classic business fashion, Indonesian carvings, renaissance paintings or science fiction books.

The thoughts and belief you allow into your brain and use on a daily basis are your internal furniture. Have you every taken a look at the style of those beliefs and asked yourself "is that what I actually want?".

We all prefer quality furniture that looks good, complements our surroundings and lasts a long time, potentially standing up to the onslaught of pets and children. That is what quality means to most of us. And yet, we don't seem to use the same rigorous approach with which we select furniture or clothing, in the selection and filtering of our thoughts.

If you think of choosing your thoughts as the same as choosing your furniture, then you can be selective about what you install and when, you can insist on only quality and robustness for lasting satisfaction, you can use it for any circumstance. It will stand up to the inspection of your friends. It might inspire them to get some new furniture in their "brain attic".

Chose what you put inside your house of thought, and at all times, insist on the best quality you can get.

Becky Paroz

DECEMBER 7

Affirmation: *Friendship with one's self is all-important because without it one cannot be friends with anyone else in the world.* —Eleanor Roosevelt

Learn to treat yourself as your own best friend. Forgive yourself, love yourself and speaking kindly to yourself.

Linda Ellis Eastman

DECEMBER 8

"It's better to walk alone than with a crowd going in the wrong direction."
—Diane Grant

A coward and a bully are promoters of negativity; their companions are otherwise known as mean spirit, nastiness and insecurity; their strength comes from the crowd that stokes them. The harmful attention and assistance they receive from others makes it possible for them feel fearless. However, when they operate alone they like to be low-keyed and remain anonymous; because on their own they become fearful that who they are will be revealed.

A champion is an explorer who has made it their personal life mission to look for something positive and valuable in everyone; their companions are also known as respect, co-existence, compassion and acceptance. – I choose to be a champion.

"To make all of your friends feel that there is something special in them."
—Optimist International Creed

Shirley A. Williams

DECEMBER 9

Affirmation: *Don't Worry - Be Happy!*—Bobby McFerrin and Bob Marley

I love this Bobby McFerrin / Bob Marley song! Here's a You-tube version if you want to listen to it! http://www.youtube.com/watch?v=L3HQMbQAWRc. It always makes me smile. The lyrics are so powerful - "When you worry, you make it double... When you worry your face will frown and that will bring everybody down...Don't Worry - Be Happy!" How true is that! Think about it. Our emotions are triggered when our expectations are not met. We view the world through the eyes of our own judgments and perspectives. When things don't go as we think they should, we get upset or our emotions are triggered. Yet, we don't always know the "whole picture." One of my former colleagues, Bobbi Brooks used to say to me when I was upset, "Kim, that's what God looks like right now." At first I would always resist and think, "This could not be God." Then later as events or emotions would unfold, I would begin to recognize the Divine Perfection and Divine Intervention. It's true with whatever we face. Sometimes the most difficult challenges, whether it's physical (such as a cancer diagnosis, ill health, heart disease, diabetes, weight or hormonal issues), psychological/emotional issues (loss of a parent or family member, loss of a job, empty nest syndrome and learning a new relationship with children who are now adults) or Spiritual aspects (The search for Truth, Am I fulfilling my Divine Purpose, What is life all about, What happens after I leave this physical body, What is beyond?) are triggers for profound growth. Instead of going to fear and upset as we are commonly conditioned, how about if we just "Don't Worry - Be Happy?" This allows us to feel the emotion, observe it, transcend it and witness Divine Intervention. You just might see the silver lining in the cloud! You might begin to see the Miraculous unfold!

Kim Evans

DECEMBER 10

Affirmation: *Learn to operate in the realm of Christ and you will be that beacon of light that will make him known.*

Psalms 119:105 *Thy word is a lamp unto my feet, and a light unto my path.*

Cassandra Gaines

DECEMBER 11

Affirmation: *Spread love everywhere you go. Let no one come to you without leaving happier.* —Mother Theresa

How will you be remembered? What is your legacy? The most valuable gift you can leave behind when you depart the earth is your kindness and love for others.

Linda Ellis Eastman

DECEMBER 12

"The death of a loved one can help you appreciate your life more fully."
—Susan Taylor

Whenever I reach a point in my life that I feel I can't go on, or that I won't reach a goal that I have set for myself, I simply think about my "cheerleaders in heaven." My cheerleaders in heaven are my sister, "Meter," my grandmother, "Ms. Lizzie," my mother, "Sweet Lucy" and my best friend, Bettie Ann. On numerous occasions while these angels were on earth, they convinced me that there was nothing I could not do if I put my mind to it. Their confidence in me and for me was unshakable no matter how impossible the task or challenge that confronted me. Therefore, when I come to a rough place or things seem to be overwhelming, I imagine these precious women cheering and encouraging me to hold on and to keep pressing on until I have reached my goal. Consequently, during trying times, I am grateful to have had them in my life. As well, I appreciate my life even more, because in spirit they continue to compel me to keep trying and never to give up regardless of the circumstances.

"Angels in heaven done signed my name."

Ann Ransom

DECEMBER 13

Affirmation: *"You gain strength, courage, and confidence by every experience in which you really stop to look fear in the face. You must do the thing you think you cannot do."* —Eleanor Roosevelt

Whatever we think, we become. If you spend your days continually thinking you cannot do something, you won't be able to do it. If you are waiting to find courage to do something you fear, it will likely not come. Doing is what moves us past our fears. Action over inaction wins out every time. If you consistently pursue steps to overcome the things you think you cannot do, you will eventually accomplish your goals. Every step will give you more strength, the courage you were looking for, and confidence to approach the next obstacle with tenacity. Be a doer.

Marcie Wingfield Shanks

DECEMBER 14

Affirmation: *"Success is not final, failure is not fatal: it is the courage to continue that counts."* —Winston Churchill

We have often been taught that when things do not work out a certain way, we have failed. If our marriage ended in a divorce or if we did not live up to our dreams, we see ourselves as failures.

This is a perception that does not benefit us. Life is a journey full of ups and downs; challenges and joys. Our job is to maneuver through this journey of life to learn as much as we can and enjoy it. However, our thoughts often try to tell us that we are on the wrong path or that life dealt us a curve ball. Instead, if we take every situation as an opportunity to learn and grow, we are a step ahead of the game because there is no judgement of right or wrong. It just is. Strive for a homerun.

This state of mind gives us the courage to put one foot in front of the other because we can now view life as an adventure rather than be fearful of the outcome.

Ask yourself today, "What adventure will I encounter today?"

Maritza Rodriguez-Arseneau

DECEMBER 15

"Remove those 'I want you to like me' stickers from your forehead and, instead, place them where they truly will do the most good — on your mirror!" —Susan Jeffers

Greet each morning with enthusiasm.

Starting each day with a happy mind sets me off on the right course. You jump out of bed eager to see what lies ahead.

Being a morning person is a choice I make. I develop rituals that encourage you to smile as soon as you open your eyes.

You keep inspirational quotes and pictures near your bed. I slip your feet into bunny slippers. Drinking in the morning light rouses your senses, so you draw back the curtains to make it easier for you to get moving.

Every hour is precious to you. You want to be productive. You want to be cheerful and alert before noon. There are many opportunities to learn and grow before lunch. You want to be ready to seize them.

It all starts the night before with getting a good night's rest. Stick to a regular schedule. Shut off the TV and computer in the early evening so you are relaxed and ready to sleep. Give yourself plenty of time to prepare for the day ahead and be realistic about how long it takes to get the kids ready for school and walk the dog.

Affirmation: *Today, I look forward to the morning light. There is so much to love about mornings. I appreciate sunrises, bird songs, and waffles. I start out energetically and carry that zeal with me throughout the day.*

Judith Duclot-Fletcher

DECEMBER 16

Surrounding yourself by supporting and loving people can make a huge difference in your life. It is important to know who is "good for you" and to eliminate those who are not. Look around your life and pick out the 3-5 people who have a track record of loving you and caring about your outcome. Let's call this group your Personal Board of Directors or PBoD. Your PBoD is your go-to committee. Every successful human being should have a PBoD. Currently, my husband is the head of my PBoD.

On the eve of our anniversary, I would like to point out why I have appointed him to that position.

- He respects my goals and dreams.
- He supports my career ambition.
- He wants to be in the seat next to me, sometimes as the pilot, sometimes as the co-pilot. He doesn't mind changing seats.
- He makes me feel like superwoman. I can accomplish anything.
- He encourages me to take risks.
- He provides a gentle landing spot when I fall.
- He doesn't judge me when I make mistakes.
- He listens. He truly listens empathically and at a higher level.
- He makes me feel safe to be me.
- He calls my bluff.
- He knows my faults and loves me because of them.
- He challenges me to grow.
- He is not threatened by my success.
- He is committed to his own growth and to the growth of our relationship.

Who is on your PBoD? Who needs to be removed? What would you be capable of accomplishing if you had a loving support system?

Jill Johns

DECEMBER 17

"A friend is someone who gives you total freedom to be yourself."
—Jim Morrison

True Friends are hard to come by. They are often developed over time but fast friends are quickly made through a connection of kindred hearts. My dad always told me that there is a difference between friends and acquaintances. It is extremely important to know the difference. True friends set themselves apart from acquaintances. You would not divulge a secreto an acquaintance but you probably would to a true friend.

A true friend loves and embraces all that you are and hope to be; gives you space when you need it; is objective with their advice; and is concerned about your well-being. A true friend celebrates you for who you are and your accomplishments. A true friend is lovingly honest with you and gives you constructive, helpful feedback. A true friend cares about you and understands what is important to you and offers you the support you need. We all need these kinds of people in our lives.

Be inspired to nurture friendships that empower you to be the best that you can be.

Affirmation: *I will be a true friend.*

Frenetta Tate

DECEMBER 18

"It is more blessed to give than to receive." —Jesus

"We make a living by what we get, but we make a life by what we give."
—Dave Ramsey

I want to think I have a giving heart, charitable thoughts and be pure of heart & mind. Also, I want to see charity in all that I do my interactions with others and in my plans for the future. Where do I look for reassurance for this?

The reality is I have a giving heart and I take stock of this character trait every day. My actions speak to this reality each moment of every day. If I need reassurance, my family, friends and my God reassure me daily.

I have charitable thoughts for those that have shown me charity in our day to day interactions.

And for those that I feel compassion for one reason or another, I am overt in my charitable actions. This is also proven in my actions with my loved ones. They are overwhelming in their commentary so I have no need to wonder.

I look to God to back up the pure of heart and mind as I seem to speak with him often of my thoughts, dreams and desires. He reassures me I am just where I need to be to be the woman he molded me into over the last 45 years.

He also opens up the door and says in a charitable tone, I will be more blessed over the next few years so that I may bless others with my charity. This is all the reassurance I need!

Michele McLeskey

DECEMBER 19

"Never underestimate the power of a woman." —Nellie McClung

Your life goals are worth my efforts.

I live my life in a way that pleases me. **My choices benefit me and move me closer toward accomplishing my life goals.** I take charge of my future in order for my dreams to become my reality.

I have a responsibility to myself to fulfill my dreams because I am the only person with the power to do so.

My daily responsibilities facilitate my ultimate life goals because my life surrounds and supports those goals. Sure, organizing my life in this manner takes time and effort, but pursuing my goals is a noble endeavor, worthy of my time and effort.

My family's happiness and wellbeing are major parts of my life goals. My family motivates me to continue my pursuit of happiness and it makes me happy to serve them as well.

I am focused on achieving my goals.

Each day, I work hard and play just as intensely, but I always take time to take a step toward my goals. My decisions are geared toward fulfilling them. And my goals are the first thing I think about each morning when I awake and plan my day.

My goals are worth my efforts because they are important to me. I dedicate myself to achieving them.

Affirmation: *Today, I am committed to making my dreams come true. I create goals and work toward them diligently. I continue to invest my time and energy because my life goals are worth my efforts.*

Judith Duclot-Fletcher

DECEMBER 20

Get excited about what can go right, not wrong!

Today is a day when most families are actively in the hustle and bustle of the holiday season. Well, let's face it, it's probably mostly the women who are running franticly around making sure every last detail of their family celebrations is just right. Did I make enough cookies? Did I pull the turkey out to thaw in time? Are the guest bedroom sheets clean? Do the kids have clean outfits to wear? Did I remember everyone on my gift list? It is at this time of year that I often want it all to just stop. In my efforts to make everything perfect, I can easily get so stressed that I become the last person my family wants to be around! And that does not make for an enjoyable celebration. Not for them and certainly not for me.

So this year, I commit to change: I will stop worrying about what can go wrong, and get excited about what can go right.

By doing so, maybe the turkey will have to go into the oven from frozen. Maybe the kids won't be donned in their Sunday-best. And maybe we don't need all those cookies anyway! But what could go right is the way we connect as a family, and the memories of happiness we get to make together. That's worth getting excited about! Don't you agree?

Rebecca Sheperd

DECEMBER 21

Affirmation: *"It had long since come to my attention that people of accomplishment rarely sat back and let things happen to them. They went out and happened to things."* —Leonardo da Vinci

Everybody has heard of Leonardo da Vinci. He needs no introduction. He was a man who was famous for his ideas and his creations. His works of art are still amongst the best in the world today.

He knew that he made his own success and that his ideas would live on beyond his lifetime. He didn't wait for the recognition he deserved, he just got on with the process of being as fabulous as he could within his environment.

Do you sit back and wait for things to happen to you? Are you still waiting to be recognized for your career efforts, your contribution to your children's upbringing? Do you keep saying "one day I will be recognized".

Stop waiting. No-one will hand you the success you are looking for, you need to make it happen. Make a choice, here and now, to get amongst life. Give yourself the recognition you deserve, don't wait for someone else to give you the permission to be the fabulous you, that you know you are.

Get out and happen to life, let life know you are about to 'bring it' and don't wait for life to happen to you.

Becky Paroz

DECEMBER 22

*"There will always be reasons why you meet people…Either you need them
to change your life or you're the one who will change theirs."*
—"Lessons Learned In Life"

I have learned some invaluable life lessons and experienced personal growth from every person whose life has touched mine. Each encounter has presented a challenge or an opportunity for me to focus on creating an environment for me to think about the positive impact I can make on the lives of others. (And the positive impact they could possibly make on my life.)

Once I got it, I and embraced looking at it from that perspective, it enabled me to change my life outlook and in some instances it changed the other person's point of view on life as well. Changing me was a revelation that equipped me to say to others with conviction, "I accept you for who you are now". I now understand the importance of "meeting people where they are", doing so liberates us from the burden of believing that we have the power to change anyone other than ourselves.

"If someone shows you their true colors, don't try to repaint them."
—Raw For Beauty.com

Shirley A. Williams

DECEMBER 23

I listen deep
to the songs of the angels.

It has been said, in times gone by, that the veil between Heaven and Mother Earth is so very thin this time of year, this time of Winter and her winter solstice with many lovely celebrations around the world.

In my many years on this earth, I have come to believe that to be so. For I have experienced some miracles right before my own eyes, precious and priceless ones. Miracles that years ago I may never have noticed, may have just totally overlooked, too busy or too self-indulgent to be aware of the ethereal beauty that surrounds all of us this December.

As a child I remembered the beauty of a living tree all adorned in the living room of my mama and daddy's little cottage house. Only the tree lights sparkled in the darkness. The pine scent was intoxicating. The child in me could feel the magical, the mystical, the miraculous energy that embraces this time of year.

And, now in my wisdom years, I allow myself to have that experience again. I give myself the quiet space and time, a fire in the fireplace, candles lit, my Norwegian pine with her twinkling golden lights shimmering.

I sit in the darkness, in the silence
allowing the mystery of this time of year
to wash over me.

I listen deep, knowing the angels are singing right to me.
in this magnificent, gentle moment out of time
when Heaven is close to Mother Earth.

Sharon McWilliams

DECEMBER 24

"If your compassion does not include yourself it is incomplete." —Buddha

You should be the first person that you fall in love with. Loving you and taking care of yourself is not selfish; in fact it is the foundation that helps us build the capability to pass love on. Failing to do so is being careless about doing what is in your own best interest. I equate self compassion with love; if I don't value, love, consider and care for myself and my own needs, how can I share such a special gift with others? When you show evidence of self compassion and love for yourself, you provide an example of your expectations from others; and you create an atmosphere for it to thrive in.

"Some people create their own storms, and then get upset when it rains"
—Unknown

Shirley A. Williams

DECEMBER 25

Affirmation. *Step out of the box*

Are you living your dreams? Have you found your passion? Do you think you have anything special to offer someone in this world? Have you been told all of your life you wouldn't amount to a hill of beans? Has someone defined you by their opinion. Isn't it just an opinion? We all get to have one, and its O.K. It doesn't mean what someone projects on us is true. Remember it's just an opinion. We are all here to step out of the box, be the unique people we are and shine, shine, shine! What are you waiting for? There is a genius and creative soul in every one of us. Be fearless to show your talent and be an inspiration for others and those around you. You will be so proud of yourself. Plus you have what someone wants. What are you waiting for? Life is pretty short. Don't waste another minute. Get to work! The world is waiting for your specialty and uniqueness. Surprise us and show us what you've got. You will be so happy to give back to the world. You will feel GREAT about yourself. It's in each and every one of us. Find what you are here to do. (Just do it) Nike says it best. Inspire! Let's celebrate this Christmas day with giving.

LOVE YOURSELF.

Angie Schultz

DECEMBER 26

Affirmation: *"The power is in you!"*

We are all born equal. The power seed is in all of us. The question is how this seed will be nourished. We can learn from the positive and make it better. We can also learn from the negative and make sure we will change our pattern and decrease any undesirable impact.

Use your power to empower others around you and they in turn will pay it forward and empower others and so on. Thus we can help ourselves and the make the world a better place at the same time.

There is no better feeling than the service of giving. Try it, feel it, live it.

Maritza Rodriguez-Arseneau

DECEMBER 27

"Women have to harness their power – it's absolutely true. It's just learning not to take the first no. And if you can't go straight ahead, you go around the corner." —Cher

You are more than a woman.

When you open your eyes each morning, realize that you are more than your gender, more than your emotions, and more than your natural ability as nurturer. You are more than a woman.

Believe that your womanhood symbolizes strength. Being a woman makes you able to meet tough challenges head on without fear or doubt. *You are stronger than any label the world tries to pin on me.*

Know that your womanhood epitomizes brilliance. You are a creator, definer, and maker of great things. You can envision endless possibilities and turn those possibilities into realities. Nothing you set my brilliant mind on is out of your reach.

You are the carrier of burdens for your family and loved ones. You are the listening ear, the open arms and the strong shoulder for tears of sadness to roll down onto. You lift them up in their times of despair. *You are a channel through which good things flow.*

Affirmation: *Today, I celebrate my indefinable status. I am inspired by something greater than the labels that society may want to place on me. The sky is my limit and I use every opportunity to show I am capable of reaching the stars.*

Judith Duclot-Fletcher

DECEMBER 28

Any man who can drive safely while kissing a pretty girl is simply not giving the kiss the attention it deserves. —Albert Einstein

A happy family is but an earlier heaven. —George Bernard Shaw

I met Margaret in 2000 when I changed jobs, company & states. Suffice it to say she treated me with respect, kindness and friendship from day one. She has displayed integrity, honor and grace throughout our entire friendship. She has changed jobs multiple times as have I and we still remain friends. Today it is more like close friends that mentor-mentee.

As we have aged, our jobs have taken us into different directions so as we grow in our jobs our lives were turned upside down for one reason or another. Through it all, she has displayed grace under fire as we were individually attacked by one nefarious faction after another. We have shared confidences for years and it all that time. She has proven to me that Focus plus Family equals success at every turn!

I am forever in her debt for her strength of character. She has shown me that true success is focusing on your family while striving for professional success. For this, I will be vigilant in my pursuit of family, love and success!

Michele McLeskey

DECEMBER 29

Affirmation: *I lovingly care for my body.*

"All true healing takes place from within. Know your body, listen to your body, love your body, nourish your body - and your body will heal itself."
—Dr. Edward Group III

When you have a glass of water, if you keep emptying it out without replenishing the supply, you end up with an empty glass. If you leave the water without replenishing the supply, it will stagnate.

The same principles apply to your body and your health. If you take your body for granted, push it to its limits without replenishing it with healthy food, rest, recreation and exercise, you risk your health and well-being. Similarly, when you criticize your body for not being the ideal shape, size, or fitness level, you are coming from judgement instead of love.

Your body is the only one you have and it has amazing capabilities. It is the vehicle that allows you to travel through life. Love your body, treat it with respect and show it gratitude. It will love you back.

Janet Christensen

DECEMBER 30

Affirmation: *"Live each and every day as if it were your last-because one day you'll be right."* —Bob Mowad

Every day that you wake up is a good day full of new opportunities, possibilities and adventures. You have the ability to capture and treasure each moment. Life can be extraordinary; don›t miss it! Savor every moment.

Carpe diem is commonly known as 'seize the day'. Wikipedia defines carpe diem as 'enjoy the day' or 'pluck the day [as it is ripe]'. Each definition is wonderful:

- Seize - take hold of and grasp
- Enjoy - like, take pleasure in and benefit from
- Pluck - courage, backbone and fortitude

Whether you ‹seize the day›, 'enjoy the day› or ‹pluck the day [as it is ripe]›, the day has the possibility of being remarkable, astounding and miraculous. Every day is a gift; unwrap and treasure it. What is on your ‹bucket list›? Today is the day to begin work on the goals and dreams that you desire to accomplish.

Live life to the fullest; the choice is uniquely yours. Carpe diem!

Lori Tsugawa Whaley

DECEMBER 31

Affirmation: *"Happy new year!"*

Have you made your New Years resolution? This is the time to think about your New Year and think, what can I change? What can make me a better me? How can I get more organized? Who can I give my old things to? How can I inspire myself to be an inspiration for others? A new year to change, be grateful, be more generous, and be more balanced. Forgive yourself and get in the present. Leave the past behind. Learn from it and move on. Start anew. Are you being the best mother, the best co-worker, and the best friend? Are you accountable, hard working, and honest? Continue to ask yourself these questions. There is always room to be better. Are you being the best person you can be when no one is watching? Stay in the moment and enjoy the process. Count your blessings. Follow no one, but learn from everyone. When you change your mind, you change your life.

Angie Schultz

Contributing authors for The Woman's Book of Empowerment &
Confidence: 365 Daily Affirmations

Linda Ellis Eastman	Becky Paroz
Rev. Kymberley Clemons Jones	Angie Schultz
Michele McLeskey	Lori Whaley
Gabriela Eikeland	Marcie Wingfield Shanks
Judy Singleton	Jill Johns
Rebecca Sheperd	Sharon McWilliams
Frenetta Tate	Dr. Joanne Siebert
Dr. Katrina Everhart	Judith Fletcher
Barbara Bowes	Cassandra Gaines
Janet Christensen	Donna Anderson
Maritza Rodriguez-Arseneau	Dr. Betty Shadrick
Shirley Williams	Dana Cable
Michelle Richardson	Kim Evans
Ann Ransom	Paula Onysko
Dawn Jamison	
Mary Romero	Foreword by
	Amicitia Maloon Gibson

THE PROFESSIONAL WOMAN NETWORK
Training and Certification on Women's Issues

Linda Ellis Eastman, President & CEO of The Professional Woman Network, has trained and certified over two thousand individuals to start their own consulting/seminar business. Women from such countries as Brazil, Argentina, the Bahamas, Costa Rica, Bermuda, Nigeria, South Africa, Malaysia, and Mexico have attended trainings.

Topics for certification include:
• Diversity & Multiculturalism
• Women's Issues
• Women: A Journey to Wellness
• Save Our Youth
• Teen Image & Social Etiquette
• Leadership & Empowerment Skills for Youth
• Customer Service & Professionalism
• Marketing a Consulting Practice
• Professional Coaching
• Professional Presentation Skills

If you are interested in learning more about becoming certified or about starting your own consulting/seminar business contact:

The Professional Woman Network
P.O. Box 333
Prospect, KY 40059
(502) 566-9900
lindaeastman@prodigy.net
www.prowoman.net

Women's Empowerment Series

Creating a Blue Print for Inner Change: Tools for Personal Growth
Tapping into Your Inner CEO Self-Leadership
Leaders in Pearls: Becoming a Change Architect
Releasing Strongholds: Letting Go of What is Holding You Back
The Power of a Woman: Embracing the Woman Within
How to Break the Glass Ceiling Without a Hammer
The Power of Change: Reinvent Yourself at Any Age
Life is an Attitude. The Power of Positive Thinking
Transformation: Reinventing the Woman Within
Learning to Love Yourself: Self-Esteem for Women
A Journey Within: Self-Discovery for Women
The Woman's Handbook for Self-Confidence
Remove the Mask! Living an Authentic Life
The Woman's Handbook for Self-Empowerment
Becoming Your Own Best Friend
The Self-Architect: Redesigning Your Life

The African American Library

Single and Loving It! Secrets for the SINGLE African American Sister
Boys to Men The Guide for African American Boys
Sister to Sister A Guide for African American Girls
Bruised But Not Broken
Learning to Love Yourself: A Handbook for the African American Woman
Wellness for the African American Woman: Mind, Body & Spririt
Life Skills for the African American Woman
Raising African American Boys
Raising African American Girls
Living Your Vision and Purpose

The Professional Woman Network - Book Series
Becoming the Professional Woman
Customer Service & Professionalism for Women
Self-Esteem & Empowerment for Women
The Young Woman's Guide for Personal Success
The Christian Woman's Guide for Personal Success
Survival Skills for the African-American Woman
Overcoming the SuperWoman Syndrome
You're on Stage! Image, Etiquette, Branding & Style
Women's Journey to Wellness: Mind, Body & Spirit
A Woman's Survival Guide for Obstacles, Transition & Change
Women as Leaders: Strategies for Empowerment & Communication
Beyond the Body! Developing Inner Beauty
The Young Man's Guide for Personal Success
Emotional Wellness for Women Volume I
Emotional Wellness for Women Volume II
Emotional Wellness for Women Volume III
The Baby Boomer's Handbook for Women

Youth Empowerment Series
Raising Healthy Children in an Unhealthy World
The Teen Handbook for Self-Confidence

These books are available from the individual contributors, the publisher (www.pwnbooks.com), www.amazon.com, and your local bookstore by request.